14⁰⁰

D1222885

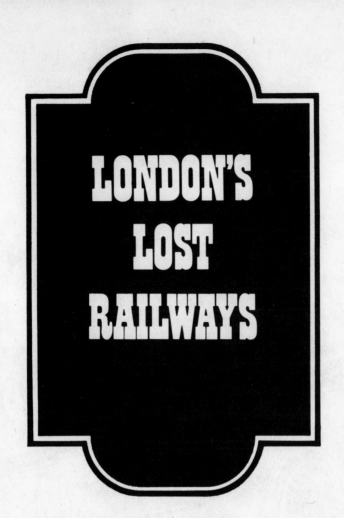

LONDON'S LOST RAILWAYS

Charles Klapper

LONDON'S LOST RAILWAYS

Routledge & Kegan Paul

London, Henley and Boston

First published in 1976
by Routledge & Kegan Paul Ltd
39 Store Street,
London WC1E 7DD
Broadway House,
Newtown Road,
Henley-on-Thames,
Oxon RG9 1EN and
9 Park Street,
Boston, Mass. 02108, USA
Set in Monotype Plantin by Kelly Selwyn & Co
and printed in Great Britain by
Unwin Brothers Limited,
The Gresham Press, Old Woking, Surrey
a member of the Staples Printing Group

© Charles Klapper 1976
No part of this book may be reproduced in
any form without permission from the
publisher, except for the quotation of brief
passages in criticism

ISBN 0 7100 8378 5

CONTENTS

PLATES

Plates Between pages 66–67

Maps

ILLUSTRATIONS

Timetables

PREFACE AND ACKNOWLEDGMENTS

This book does not set out to be notable as a work of historical research; its endeavour is to contrast the railway scene of the past in the Metropolis, particularly in the heyday of steam traction, with that of the present day, to pose the background of the changes and some of the reasons for them, and to indicate some of the possible means of re-establishing extensive use of the lines on which traffic for various reasons has fallen away. A study on these lines was first proposed to me by Timothy O'Sullivan in 1973. In attempting it I have been grateful for help from many quarters, not least from my many friends in the London Transport Executive and British Railways organisations. Every writer who deals with the London scene must be conscious of the contributions made to knowledge by writers of the past, including such pioneers of railway description and historical record as G. A. Nokes (G. A. Sekon), the Rev. W. J. Scott, those stalwarts of railway literature and friends of my youth H. L. Hopwood, J. F. Gairns and Cecil J. Allen, and more currently the erudite works of Professor Theo Barker, Dr Edwin Course, Alan A. Jackson, Charles E. Lee and Michael Robbins. One is fortunate in all one's friends and particularly in the case of the present work for the assistance given by H. V. Borley and Michael Robbins in criticising various passages. Responsibility for errors and opinions is nevertheless my own. I am also indebted to a number of photographers for assistance in illustrating the subject matter so cogently, especially the courteous provision of views from the Ian Allan Collection, the repertoire of H. C. Casserley's London views and the generous provision of delightful prints by Dick Riley. British Railways and London Transport have also provided photographs with their usual efficiency and Peter Gerhold and W. H. R. Godwin have supplied shots of particular interest to this study.

Plates 14, 24, 32 and 35 are reproduced from photographs by the author.

Other plates are reproduced by kind permission of the following: Aero Pictorial Ltd: 1; John F. Ayland: 22; British Railways, London

Midland Region: 16, 17, 18, 19, 20, 21; Bucknall Collection/Ian Allan Ltd: 6, 7; H. C. Casserley: 13, 26, 27, 29; W. H. R. Godwin: 33; Ian Allan Ltd: 9, 31, 37, 41; G. D. King: 42; R. K. Kirkland: 30; London Transport Executive: 36, 38, 39, 40; Museum of British Transport, York: 2, 3, 4, 5, 43; and R. C. Riley: 10, 11, 12, 15, 23, 25, 28.

I should also like to pay a tribute of appreciation and praise to my wife, for her helpful criticisms and for her valuable work of indexing.

C.F.K.

ABBREVIATIONS

It has been convenient to refer to railways at various points of this book by their pre-grouping or pre-nationalisation titles or initials; a key to the latter therefore follows:

BR	British Railways
CC, E & H	Charing Cross, Euston & Hampstead Railway (now Northern Line)
CCR	Charing Cross Railway (now Southern Region)
CLR	Central London Railway (now Central Line)
C & SLR	City & South London Railway (now Northern Line)
ELR	East London Railway (now section of Metropolitan Line)
GCR	Great Central Railway (London area now Western Region)
GER	Great Eastern Railway (now Eastern Region)
GN & CR	Great Northern & City Railway (now Northern City branch of Northern Line and to be transferred to Eastern Region of British Railways operation in 1976)
GN, P & B	Great Northern, Piccadilly & Brompton (Piccadilly Line)
GNR	Great Northern Railway (now Eastern Region)
GWR	Great Western Railway (now Western Region)
HJR	Hampstead Junction Railway (now London Midland Region)
L & BR	London & Birmingham Railway (now London Midland Region)
	London & Blackwall Railway (now Eastern Region)
LB & SCR	London, Brighton & South Coast Railway (now Southern Region)
LC & DR	London, Chatham & Dover Railway (now Southern Region)
L & CR	London & Croydon Railway (now Southern Region)

L & GR	London & Greenwich Railway (now Southern Region)
LMSR	London, Midland & Scottish Railway (now London Midland Region)
LNER	London & North Eastern Railway (now Eastern Region)
LNWR	London & North Western Railway (now London Midland Region)
LPTB	London Passenger Transport Board (now London Transport Executive)
LSWR	London & South Western Railway (now Southern Region)
LTE	London Transport Executive
LTSR	London, Tilbury & Southend Railway (now Eastern Region)
MET	Metropolitan (now London Transport Metropolitan Line)
MR	Midland Railway (now London Midland Region)
MSWJ	Midland & South Western Junction (Cricklewood–Acton) (now London Midland Region)
NLR	North London Railway (London Midland Region)
SE & CR	South Eastern & Chatham Railways Managing Committee (now Southern Region)
SER	South Eastern Railway (now Southern Region)
SHLR	Southern Heights Light Railway (not built)
SR	Southern Railway (now Southern Region)
T & HJR	Tottenham & Hampstead Junction (later Joint) Railway
W & CR	Waterloo & City Railway (now Southern Region)
WLER	West London Extension Railway (joint LNW, GW, LB & SC, LSW)
WLR	West London Railway (joint LNWR and GWR)

one

INTRODUCTION

London is a city of great contrasts and this even applies to its railway systems. There are the differing philosophies behind the service and fare structure of the London Transport railways and those of British Railways. With the routes of British Railways there are the sharp distinctions between the radial routes, busy with Inter City, outer suburban services, probably in 1975 to a greater extent than ever before, and peripheral and cross-town routes, with their languishing or vanished passenger services and the lesser use made of them for freight with the rationalisation of goods traffic made possible by the nationalisation of the main railway system, the fall in domestic coal traffic, the introduction of block train handling, and the rise of motor haulage. The number of wagons passing across London has been reduced by 80 per cent in the last quarter of a century. The result has been that some sections of railway are under-used, some have been abandoned, and others are under threat of joining those already disused.

Examples of the under-utilisation include the Widened Lines of the Metropolitan to Moorgate, the Fenchurch Street branch between Gas Factory and Bow junctions, used only for depot purposes, and the remaining freight links between the north of the Thames lines and the Southern Region – that is, the West London and West London Extension Railways and the North & South Western Junction Railway and its connections. Relegated to peak hour or other exceptional use are the London Transport lines between Aldwych and Holborn and between Earl's Court and Kensington Olympia. Abandonment has been the fate of the Edgware, Highgate & London Railway between Finsbury Park and Wellington Sidings, Highgate, over what was once the busiest of Great Northern suburban lines in the Northern Heights, now so embodied in the rural environment in the midst of a great city that a scheme for building several hundred dwellings in the cutting has been turned down by popular acclaim. A similar effect can be observed on the mutilated remains of the erstwhile Crystal Palace & South London

[2]

Junction Railway between Nunhead and the former elaborate terminus at Crystal Palace, while the companion branch of the London, Chatham & Dover, to Greenwich Park, has been utterly obliterated over long sections. The Woodside & South Croydon Railway, used from 1935 for a rather roundabout electric service to Sanderstead and recently relegated to peak hours only operation, is one of the lines under threat. The Metropolitan Watford branch beyond Croxley comes into this category, supposing the eminently sensible proposal of joining it to the BR Croxley Green branch were adopted to take Metropolitan trains into Watford High Street and Watford Junction could be adopted. This rouses echoes of the Metropolitan's own efforts to reach the High Street of Watford, which resulted in the construction of a typical Metropolitan station building on a High Street frontage, used for a restaurant and later as shop premises, but to which the somewhat hesitantly projected railway access was never consummated.

That is what this book is about. Some account is given of the many extraordinary non-radial services, especially passenger services, that flourished in the nineteenth century and into the early years of the twentieth century until the First World War brought the competing railway companies to their senses and to a better appreciation of the competition they rather hopelessly faced as soon as their routes were not the most direct and speedy way of traversing London. Attention is devoted to the many brave schemes for London area railways that were never achieved and especially to the pros and cons of peripheral routes, including the many schemes for outer circle railways as opposed to outer circle train services, ring rail, bypasses for freight round London and similar arrangements. There is an examination of schemes for the new use of lines, if ever a Government has the courage to invest in urban railways as radial routes for London Transport purposes. In case any reader has a lingering feeling for expenditure to be devoted to circular routes, there are cogent comparisons with realistic outlooks in Continental countries on the relative merits of spending money on radial lines of suburban communication and on circular services, in which indirect services seem to be heavy losers.

two

AS
THINGS
WERE

The Victorian and Edwardian railways gave an impression of intense bustle – in London alone there were eleven main-line terminating railways at the end of the nineteenth century, plus three local railways with their own rolling stock and locomotives in addition to the dock company's lines. Separate ownerships not only made for a variety of motive power and carriage stock but also for a variety of freight movements, some of considerable complexity. A cheerful volume of noise emission also characterised the scene. The welkin rang under the echoing overall roofs of the great termini with the beat of Westinghouse pumps on both sides of Victoria, at London Bridge, and with the hush and thump of the same apparatus – in Great Eastern style – at Liverpool Street. The continuous brake apparatus was indeed a more noticeable contributor of sound impressions than the exhaust notes of the motive power itself. At Paddington the explosive plomp of vacuum pumps of Swindon make was noticeable as shunting engines moved; at Broad Street the tall chimneys of North London Adams 4–4–0 tanks made organ pipe resonance for the ejectors of the vacuum brakes; steam brakes, less sensitive in control, could jam the wheels to stop a locomotive with a roaring slide. Four-wheel coaches, still to be the rule for many years of passenger service on the North London and much in evidence, with six-wheelers elsewhere, especially on suburban operations, made a clatter over points and crossings and rail joints unknown to modern rail fans.

Then the services included not only the radial routes of today but a great many circuitous runs through the suburbs so roundabout that a decent horse cab could beat the train. The public had been slow to embrace train travel for short journeys and the conviction that George Stephenson was right in saying that the time would come when it was cheaper to ride by train than to wear out shoeleather took a long time to soak in, although the cheap workmen's fares introduced on the Metropolitan in 1864 and by the London, Chatham & Dover in the following year, as well as more generally after the Cheap Trains Act of 1883, had much to do with popularising train travel as compared with walking to work. Even in the 1930s the elderly, conservative and fit among the population tended to regard walking as the superior method except in inclement weather rather than use train, tram or bus, the reduced fare before 0800 being unable to induce their patronage.

By the end of the nineteenth century, however, the use of the railway had become established, with the horse tram as the second-best method of travel to work and the horse bus nowhere except in the tramless western and north-western districts. While the tramway companies provided cheap workmen's return tickets, bus operators very often made little attempt in the districts served by tram to provide any early morning service and came on the roads after 0830; even as late as 1920 the first bus from Raynes Park on a London service ran after 0900.

In the days before the electric tramcar and the motor bus and before the tube railways and the electrified underground had provided short cuts across the ponderously traversed meandering routes of the steam railways a series of 'long-way-round' suburban services flourished, along with a number of connecting links between radial routes, and vestigial remains of former services. These routes made great use of the link lines built for transfer of freight from one main-line company to another, such as the West London and West London Extension Railways, the North London Railway, the Widened Lines of the Metropolitan and the connection with the London, Chatham & Dover Railway, the North & South Western Junction, what was originally the Midland & South Western Junction, the Hampstead Junction, the Tottenham & Hampstead Junction and the Tottenham & Forest Gate. It is also among these connecting railways that principal casualties among passenger railways in the London area are to be found.

The first-mentioned of the connecting railways dates back to the earliest days of railways, having been formed as the Birmingham, Bristol & Thames Junction Railway, when it was designed to join the London & Birmingham and the Bristol & London Railways (a name used chauvinistically by the Bristol promoters of the Great Western) with the Kensington Canal, which joined the Thames at Chelsea. It took up the West London title in 1840 and operated its first passenger service between May and November 1844. The full story is told in *The West London Railway and the WLER* by H. V. Borley and R. W. Kidner, but for our purposes it is sufficient to say that for eighteen years the potentialities of the line remained dormant, although it was at first leased by and then vested in the London & North Western and Great

[7]

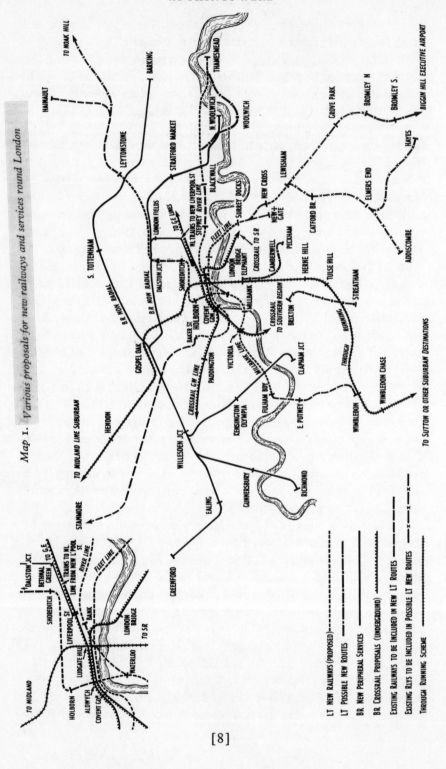

Map I. *Various proposals for new railways and services round London*

LT New Railways (Proposed) ---·---·---
LT Possible New Routes ————————
BR New Peripheral Services ————————
BR Crossrail Proposals (Underground) —————
Existing Railways to be Included in New LT Routes —————
Existing Rlys to be Included in Possible LT New Routes —x—x—x—
Through Running Scheme ————————

Western companies jointly. The 1862 International Exhibition at Kensington made a sound reason for reopening and there was a service from Harrow (for many years the first station out of Euston on the LNWR main line) and connections from North London trains at Chalk Farm or Camden. The following year these trains ran from Euston. But in that year the WL gained an exit to the south by the completion of the West London Extension Railway to join the London & South Western, London, Brighton & South Coast and London, Chatham & Dover Railways in the Clapham Junction and Longhedge area. The first two, the LSWR and the LBSCR, joined the GW and LNW, partners in the West London, in the new venture, which was completed with 7 ft gauge track. This, to suit the Great Western's eccentricity, was extended on to the Victoria Station & Pimlico's property and to the east side of Victoria Station. It is interesting that the LSW and LBSC provided Clapham Junction for the WLER interchange in 1863, but the LNWR did not get round to Willesden Junction at the north end of the WL until 1866 and the Great Western did not at any time think an exchange station with the West London was necessary; perhaps that was why its through services were unsuccessful.

New train services followed in great profusion. On 2 March 1863 the LNWR provided trains from Harrow and Camden to Kensington, whence the LBSCR took them on to Crystal Palace and the platforms at East Croydon then designated New Croydon. Later the LBSCR provided a service from Kensington to West Croydon and the Camden trains were provided through from Euston, where Brighton coaches began to appear on some of the trains. Also from the opening the LSWR operated trains from Clapham Junction to Kensington. From the Great Western, trains began from Southall to Victoria (LC & D) over the WLER on 1 April 1863. Broad gauge operation to Victoria had ceased by the autumn of 1866 and by 1875 even for freight traffic to Chelsea Basin; what a lot GW shareholders paid for Brunel's services!

The spur from Latimer Road on the Hammersmith & City line to the West London was used from 1 July 1864 by carriages detached from GW Farringdon to Hammersmith trains at the junction, and some local services from Notting Hill, as Ladbroke Grove station was then known, to Kensington, to the name of which the definitive 'Addison Road' was added in 1868 when the Metropolitan Kensington High Street was opened. Addison Road was then the best-known thoroughfare in the neighbourhood of the station and the most built up, although later it seemed a strange choice of suffix.

The Metropolitan District company in 1866 made a junction between its branch from Earl's Court and the West London Extension at West Brompton for use of construction trains; it also had in mind the prospects of persuading the LBSC and LSW companies of the merits of using the District as an alternative terminus, but this failing, the junction was soon taken out. Powers for a junction at West Brompton, with a view to traffic from the southern companies, were renewed until 1893. The MDR built a dual-purpose line in 1869, to join its line through Earl's Court and the point where the West London and West London Extension made their end-on-junction for spoil to go to dumping grounds off the West London line. Ulterior motive in the building of this line was undoubtedly the attraction of traffic from the LNWR, but its first purpose was fulfilled by mid-1870; nevertheless 'facilities to the LNWR' were among the objects of the Metropolitan District (Southern Lines) and this connection was sanctioned in the District's original Act.

Use of the spur for passenger trains began on 1 February 1872, with the beginning of the 'Outer Circle' service from Broad Street, NLR, to Mansion House on the Metropolitan District. It was operated by LNWR engines and rolling stock (for which varnished teak livery was adopted when the effects of the smoky tunnels of the underground were appreciated) at half-hourly intervals and was accompanied by a Willesden Junction (Low Level) to Victoria (LBSC) service, which succeeded endeavours from 1865 onwards to establish a Euston to South Western or South Eastern connection, running over the spur from the WLER to the LSWR at West London Junction, via Waterloo, the connection to the South Eastern and thence to London Bridge or Cannon Street; these were finally abandoned in early 1868 after only a month's trial of a shortened version from Euston to Waterloo. LNWR and LSWR rolling stock, with engine changes at Kensington, took part in this effort.

Another service over the Addison Road–Earl's Court link was the Middle Circle. This began on 1 August 1872, from Moorgate Street to Mansion House, using the Metropolitan, Hammersmith & City, West London, and Metropolitan District Railways. Standard gauge GW engines were used throughout, but District coaches were used for some journeys. From 1 July 1900 the Middle Circle was cut back to work Aldgate to Earl's Court, having been extended first to Bishopsgate (now Liverpool Street) and then to Aldgate with the extension of the Metropolitan. On 1 February 1905 the service was curtailed again to run Aldgate–Kensington (Addison Road) with a view to the coming electrification of the Metropolitan and the electrification of part of the West London to cover the GW interests in its ownership for the Metropolitan and GW electric trains which were introduced gradually during the latter part of 1906, serving the station at Uxbridge Road *en route*. With an increased Metropolitan and GW service to Hammersmith, this service again was shortened on 31 October 1910 to operate between Edgware Road and Addison Road. Sunday services disappeared during the First World War in May 1918 and the Second World War put paid to the entire service when the Latimer Road spur between the GW & Metropolitan joint line and the West London suffered damage, the last service running on 19 October 1940.

The Outer Circle continued longer than the original Middle Circle service. Between Mansion House and Earl's Court Outer Circle trains were electrically hauled in December 1905, District electric locomotives having been built to haul the LNW trains over this section. But idle time by the locomotives, through the termination at Mansion House on a single track, made the arrangement uneconomic as well as occupying train paths that the District needed for its own traffic, and from 1 January 1909 the Outer Circle service ended at Earl's Court and the District no longer saw teak carriages labelled 'L & NW train' or 'Broad Street, Willesden, Kensington and Mansion House' or 'Change at Willesden for Main Line'. Similar destination and route boards were carried on the engines. From March 1912 the LNWR provided a local service only from Willesden to Earl's Court, but passengers could pursue the Outer Circle theme by changing at Willesden Junction, as long as they were not included among the hordes of ghosts reputed by comedians to have died of starvation trying to find their way out of the ramifications of that double-decked and rather bewildering station. The London & North Western included the West London in its 1911 electrification scheme and all was ready for electric trains on 1 May 1914. Alas, Oerlikon electrical equipment was slow for delivery and the LNWR electrics were only delivered in time to begin running in November. In the meantime Lots Road provided the power and the District lent some train sets, so that long after the District company's application for running powers into Addison Road was turned down by the West London committee in the first flush of the MDR discovering that it was an impecunious company which could not contribute to the upkeep of Addison Road, District coaches began to run all the way to Willesden Junction.

The LNWR Earl's Court–Willesden service survived under LMS ownership into the Second World War when bomb damage provided a reason for withdrawal after 2 October 1940. The Outer Circle concept thus gradually faded away. Curiously it had never attracted much business on Sundays and it was only in 1891 that eight services were provided each way on Sundays from Willesden to Kensington. After electrification of the District a 30-minute Sunday service was provided between Willesden and Mansion House but this was cut back to Earl's Court at the time of curtailment of the Monday–Saturday service and ceased altogether at the end of 1916, never to be revived. LNWR services to the railways on the south side of the river, apart from that via Waterloo were begun again in the 1870s and destinations included Victoria, Central Croydon, New Croydon, East Croydon, and, between 1880 and 1890 and again between 1897 and 1900, a service via Longhedge Junction and the London, Chatham & Dover Railway to Herne Hill. In 1910 there were still advertised eleven LNWR services to Victoria, five local services to East Croydon, the Sunny South Special calling only at Willesden, Addison Road and East Croydon and then going on to Brighton and Eastbourne, one via Herne Hill to SE & CR resorts, and one via Clapham Junction to LSWR resorts.

Great Western services other than the Middle Circle over the West London and WLER did not expand on any permanent basis from the initial Victoria–Southall service; these trains at various periods were extended to such points as Windsor and came to an end on 15 March 1915, except for Sunday 21 March. Great Western through trains or through carriages from time to time ran from Reading, Bristol, Wolverhampton and Birkenhead and some were through to Dover, Folkestone and Queenborough Pier, the last two in conjunction with Flushing steamers. While bound for the South-East, in 1905 and 1906, these through coaches were slipped at Southall, but on the return, they were worked over the Latimer Road spur and joined to a westbound train at Paddington. The Great Western attempts to woo South Londoners to the Wycombe line by steam railcar were unsuccessful, whether they began from Clapham Junction or Victoria. From 1 May 1904 to 27 July 1913, according to Thomas B. Peacock's *Great Western Suburban Services*, on summer Sundays a train of ordinary coaches ran from Victoria to Henley, calling at Taplow, Maidenhead and Shiplake; there was a 9-hour layover at Henley and the empty stock had to work from Old Oak Common to Victoria and back at the beginning and end of the day.

The London & South Western partner in the WLER operated a local service from its side of Clapham Junction to Kensington from 2 March 1863 and between Waterloo and Richmond, over its new line from Kensington via Shepherd's Bush, Hammersmith (The Grove), and Brentford Road (later Gunnersbury) from 1 January 1869. This line had been a matter of some controversy before authorisation and the eventual

route was extremely indirect. The latter part, of course, provided the
North & South Western Junction service of the North London with a
direct route into Richmond. The LSWR provided, also from 1 January
1869, a service from Ludgate Hill to Richmond, designed to remedy the
distance from the City to Waterloo, but as the trains wended their way
from the West London Extension line to the London, Chatham and
Dover and changed direction from south-east to north-east, south-east
again and then east and north, it must have seemed desperately roundabout compared with a horse bus from Hammersmith to Piccadilly.
Variations on these services were operated from time to time, one
between Clapham Junction and Twickenham via Kensington, Gunnersbury, Kew Bridge and Hounslow (even more kinky, if possible) lasting
for eight years from 1901 to 1909. In 1910 there were 18 trains from the
LSWR side of Clapham Junction to Addison Road; 9 from Ludgate
Hill to Richmond via Kensington and Gunnersbury, with one to the
latter point only; most of these trips took an hour for the 14¾ miles. On
weekdays there were 13 services from Waterloo to Richmond via
Kensington and one train which began at Clapham Junction for Richmond. Although even then the line was being quadrupled from Studland Road Junction to Turnham Green (opened 3 December 1911) the
LSWR train service was declining – Herbert Walker, the new general
manager of the LSWR, gave a good hard look at the suburban system
in 1912 and 1913, when he was formulating his electrification programme and decided these circuitous routes were expendable. The war
made a good opportunity for abandonment; after further reductions in
service in 1915, complete withdrawal took place and the last services
ran on 3 June 1916.

Timetable 1. *Ludgate Hill, Kensington, Richmond and Twickenham (London & South
Western)*

A curious example of railway traditionalism concerns the LSWR line to Richmond from Kensington through Turnham Green which the District began to use on 1 June 1877. The Great Western had already used this line for trains to Richmond for a short period (1 June–31 October 1870) and now nothing would content the Metropolitan but that it should have the opportunity of running this way to Richmond, in which object it succeeded with a service from Aldgate on 1 October 1877. The Great Western took over most of the working in 1894 and ran the trains from Aldgate, but much later some of the trains were still the responsibility of the Metropolitan. After electrification at the end of 1906 the Great Western cut its service short at Ladbroke Grove and a siding at that point was used for the turn-round of this shuttle, which stopped altogether on 31 December 1910. But then, just before the Second World War the Southern Railway Company rebuilt Richmond station. New hexagonal destination boards were provided as platform indicators on the terminal bays and to my delight when on an official inspection of the station I discovered that one of the sides bore the legend 'GW TRAIN TO ALDGATE'. By that time the ex-LSWR line from Kensington to Turnham Green was occupied by the combined District and Piccadilly service from Studland Road Junction and a block of flats sprawled across its former route at Shepherd's Bush.

The LSWR Kensington and Clapham Junction service was withdrawn after 19 October 1940, after which a Southern Railway service ran for Post Office Savings Bank employees as required, morning and evening on weekdays, but it was not advertised at first. Before the Second World War *Modern Transport* advocated renewed use of the West London and WLE Railways, including a service from Wimbledon via East Putney, Clapham Junction and Kensington to Willesden Junction every 20 minutes by third rail electric trains. The Southern put up an electrification scheme but was met by the LMS and GW objection that three electric trains an hour would interfere with freight services, despite the fact that on the SR the LMS freights for Norwood yards ran between nine electric trains an hour.

The LBSCR service on the West London Extension line for the most part reflects LNWR through workings such as Euston–New Croydon, begun in 1863 and terminated at Crystal Palace on 1 January 1869, when separate LBSC trains began operation from Kensington to New Croydon or, for the short period it was open, Central Croydon. Early this century there were various through workings between the LBSCR and the LNWR and GWR. The most famous was the Sunny South Special, already mentioned, especially after the LBSCR hauled the train as far as Rugby with a 4–4–2 superheater tank engine and did not have to make a water stop. A Brighton working into Paddington (I have a photograph of this train at Westbourne Park, also with a 4–4–2 tank at the head) took place from 2 July 1906 to 29 June 1907. In 1910 LBSCR workings on the WLER between Clapham Junction and Kensington numbered 26, with an extra on Saturdays. On Sundays the entire service ran from the LSWR platforms at Clapham Junction and some of the turns were provided by railmotors.

Regular passenger trains on the West London at present include since 1965 the motorail services, as far as what became in 1946 Kensington Olympia, and since 1946 the District Line services southward from there at exhibition times to Earl's Court or High Street.

The North & South Western Junction Railway, another early connecting railway, saw a variety of services. The basic North London service had opened from Islington (now Highbury) to Bow and then over the Blackwall Extension Railway from Gas Factory Junction to Stepney and Fenchurch Street on 26 September 1850. Although the route was circuitous it was a great success and the NL carried 97,000 passengers in its first week. The route was gradually extended towards the LNWR main line and then on 1 August 1853 North London trains made a big jump forward in running non-stop from Hampstead Road via the site of Willesden Junction over the NSWJR, calling at Acton to a temporary platform at Kew, or rather Brentford, near Old Kew Junction. Some other intermediate stops appeared later – for example, after 1 June 1855 NL trains called at Kilburn. Some trains ran on during 1854 from the NSWJR line to Windsor over the LSWR, but this looked likely to eat into the South Western's own business and the arrangement was short-lived. The LSWR wanted to make a direct line from the NSWJR to Richmond, but failed to obtain powers. A service from the NLR began to Richmond and Twickenham on 20 May 1858, reversing at Old Kew Junction and Barnes; on 1 February 1862 the route was slightly ameliorated by putting in curves at Kew and Barnes. The first was accompanied by platforms on the curve at Kew Bridge station. In 1864 ten trains went on to terminate at Kingston, but on 1 January 1869 when the direct line from South Acton through Gunnersbury was opened the services beyond Richmond ceased. The journey time of 90 minutes to the City must have been a deterrent. In the meantime the Hampstead Junction Railway had provided an alternative route from Camden Town to Willesden for NL trains from 2 January 1860. It enabled the lush residential area around Gospel Oak and Hampstead Heath to be served by train.

Both the Great Western and Midland Railways made use of the North & South Western Junction line for passenger services. The Great Western, which installed a link for freight between Acton and Acton Wells junction in 1877, provided a connecting passenger service from Southall to Willesden Junction (High Level) in 1888. On 1 October 1904 steam railcars took over the service, but it was not heavily patronised and, although the rail motors worked the Willesden turn in economically with the Greenford and Ealing trips, all were withdrawn in the coal strike of March 1912.

On the north side of Acton Wells junction what was promoted as the Midland & South Western Junction Railway joined, intended to connect, the new Midland main line to London at Hendon with the North & South Western Junction Railway. Over this a succession of unsuccessful train services was tried and found of no interest to the public. The first began on 3 August 1875 from Moorgate Street (Metropolitan) to Child's Hill, Dudden Hill, Harrow Road (stations built by the Midland to attract outer suburban custom) and Richmond, but unlike the circuitous North London route of 25 years before, won little patronage. On 1 February 1876 it gave place to an economical shuttle from Child's Hill. This won no medals either and on 1 May 1878 the service was again extended, this time to become St Pancras and Earl's Court, outcircling all Outer Circles. The Midland, which had financed the District link from Hammersmith to Studland Road Junction on the LSWR, mainly to gain access to coal yard sites at West Kensington and High Street, which object was achieved early in 1878, did not exercise its right to operate as far as South Kensington, a favourite District suggestion to companies in search of a terminal site. This service of Midland trains to Earl's Court ceased on 30 September 1880. It was some years before they again ventured and when they did it was with a Child's Hill to Gunnersbury connecting service, begun 1 January 1894. Even with Harrow Road renamed 'Stonebridge Park', patronage was not obtained sufficiently to justify continuance indefinitely. Dudden Hill and Stonebridge Park finally closed their doors on 1 October 1904.

Long before this a shortening of the North London route round the suburbs north of the Thames had been made by opening the new City terminus of the company at Broad Street on 31 October 1865; public services began on 1 November. Traffic on the North London, already at nearly 4 million, shot up by 1867 to over 8 million passengers. At the end of 1868 North London trains ceased to run to Fenchurch Street and thereafter for over a score of years a Great Eastern shuttle joined Bow and Fenchurch Street, ceasing in 1892, after which Bow Road Great

Eastern station was built on a new site and included a covered passage from Bow North London Station, which was cheaper than running a train service. This happily did not prevent preservation by an archaeo-logically-minded station master at Fenchurch Street of a board which read 'The Hampstead and Kew express is at the end of the platform'. The service from Broad Street via Bow began to run to Poplar on 1 August 1866 and was extended thence through Poplar (London & Blackwall station) non-stop to Blackwall on 1 September 1870. This working ceased on and from 1 July 1890, by which time the public zest for getting a steamer at Blackwall Pier had abated. But North London trains still went on beyond the platforms at Poplar to locomotive sidings and for the engines to run round the carriages on the curve of the con-necting link, terminated by buffer stops which were erected in August 1896. A visitor to Bow Works as late as 1923 reported engine destination boards for Blackwall, Fenchurch Street, Stratford and Southend still in stock.

Other North London services were radial. A connection was main-tained along the LNWR main line through Kilburn to Willesden Junction, the trains being distinguished by a 'Kilburn' board on the engine, 37 times Monday to Friday, with one less on Saturdays. From 14 December 1874 the link between the Great Northern Railway and the North London at Canonbury was available. At first it was used only for freight service and the LNWR, as principal shareholder in the North London, would not allow the North London to accommodate GNR trains at Broad Street. The GN had to make a mileage allowance for use of NL rolling stock and staff in giving the greatly needed relief to GN suburban pressures when NL passenger trains began from Broad Street to Great Northern suburban stations. The North London also claimed its proportion of through fares. The services to New Barnet and High Barnet began on 18 January and to Enfield on 1 February 1875. The North London trains to the GN lines carried third-class passengers, who had not previously been very welcome in North London trains, although they gained entry to all during 1875.

Until early in this century the Metropolitan Widened Lines and the City Extension of the London, Chatham & Dover Railway were not only busy with a succession of freight trains, but with a flow of passenger trains of two of the companies south of the Thames and two of the northern lines. From stations out as far as Hitchin suburban trains began to run from the Great Northern to the Metropolitan at Farring-don Street on 1 October 1863. In January 1866 these trains were pro-jected to Ludgate Hill and there were London, Chatham & Dover trains to King's Cross, and Great Northern with through carriages to GN suburban stations. From 1 August 1866 to midsummer 1867 there were through GN trains from Hatfield to Herne Hill, and London, Chatham & Dover trains from Herne Hill to New Barnet. During 1867 the London, Chatham & Dover worked Victoria to Barnet, but after 1 July 1867, to 17 February 1868, the construction of the Widened Lines interrupted the through services. On 1 March 1868 GN and L C & D trains operated between Victoria and Barnet and GN trains from Edgware to Ludgate Hill. On 1 June 1868 the GN service became Edgware–Loughborough and on 1 June 1869 the Edgware trains were diverted from Farringdon to Moorgate Street. On 1 April 1871 a Great Northern Victoria–Enfield service was provided, and from 1 February 1875 this was supplemented by L C & D trains over the same route. There were L C & D and GN trains from Victoria to Enfield and to New Barnet and GN trains only from the L C & D to Hatfield, High Barnet, Muswell Hill and Alexandra Palace. The L C & D ran to Muswell Hill in 1892 and 1893 only. The through services were Monday to Saturday only; on Sundays the L C & D service to Moorgate Street (begun 1 September 1871) had to be used to Aldersgate, where the passenger changed to a GN train. For the two years 1866 and 1867 the L C & D trains ran to King's Cross on Sundays.

Midland trains were exchanged with the L C & D over the Widened Lines from June 1869. An L C & D working was from Victoria (some trips from Loughborough Road) to Finchley Road and Midland trains operated from Kentish Town to Herne Hill. From October 1870 Midland trains ran from Herne Hill to Crouch Hill and from May the following year to South Tottenham. A new arrangement from 1 July 1875 provided for L C & D and Midland trains between Victoria and Hendon and for Midland trains from Victoria to South Tottenham. Whereas the trains to and from the Great Northern were withdrawn on 1 October 1907, Midland trains continued until 1 July 1908, when it was at last realised that, at such long and irregular intervals as the slow services provided, there was no point in competing with trams and buses or the new tubes over these inner London routes.

The curve between the Chatham & Dover and South Eastern Railways enabling trains to run from the Metropolitan over the L C & D to London Bridge (hence 'Metropolitan Junction' on the SE at the base of the incline from the L C & D) was opened on 1 June 1878 and the South Eastern began an exchange of trains with the Great Northern between such suburban stations as Woolwich Arsenal and Enfield, Muswell Hill and Alexandra Palace. The SE through routes died rather earlier than the corresponding services to and from L C & D stations, trains between GN stations and Woolwich Arsenal being withdrawn 1 May 1907.

The writing was on the wall for the rest of the L C & D inner area business. Borough Road, which had come into service on 1 June 1864 along with the line to Blackfriars, was closed on 1 April 1907; Grosvenor Road instituted mainly as a ticket platform, closed on 1 October 1911. The last train from Victoria to Moorgate ran on 1 April 1916 and the remaining intermediate stations from Victoria to Brixton were closed along with Camberwell and Walworth Road. Snow Hill, opened on 1 August 1874, a few months after the terminal station, was also closed at this time.

The East London Railway formed a cross-river link greatly desired by the theoreticians of Parliamentary committees, but it did not generate freight or passenger traffic to the extent hoped for because of the awkwardness of its approaches; unfortunately funds ran out before the direct tunnel to the Great Eastern Railway was completed. The tunnel made still lies beneath Bethnal Green pointing in the direction of London Fields, and Lord Claud Hamilton's enthusiasm for its completion about 1919 had no result, despite his chairmanship of both the East London and Great Eastern companies. One may suspect that clearances for standard main-line stock are somewhat tight, although the writer's brother came through the Thames Tunnel in a hospital train during the First World War. It was indeed fortunate that when Brunel designed it clearance was provided for hay carts, although the builders omitted to provide road access for carts. So it was easily converted into a railway tunnel after it had failed as a foot tunnel. A service from Wapping station at the north portal to New Cross (LBSC) began on 7 December 1869. This was supplemented by a Wapping–Old Kent Road service on 13 March 1871. The northern part of the line was at last completed under London Dock and was opened to Liverpool Street on 10 April 1876. So far these trains had been provided by the Brighton company and the LBSC's William Stroudley named the first of the Terrier 0–6–0 tanks *Wapping*. What one might call a folk memory of the original schemes to join the East London with the London & Blackwall manifested itself when the LBSCR named engines after stations on that line including *Blackwall*.

The South Eastern and the L C & D had the right to participate in the operation of the East London; the L C & D began the formation of a connection from its Crystal Palace branch in 1864 but gave up, and never joined the joint lessees, of which after 1884 it was one, with physical equipment. The South Eastern gave notice of its intention to run trains on the East London 30 June 1879; and from 1 April 1880 when a junction was completed at New Cross (South Eastern) began a service from Addiscombe Road to Liverpool Street. The Metropolitan and Metropolitan District City Lines & Extensions, intended to complete the Inner Circle, was at last under construction in 1882, when the East London obtained an Act on 10 August 1882 for a junction at Whitechapel. This Act which provided also for the joint leasing of the ELR by the Brighton, South Eastern, District, Metropolitan and Chatham companies at £30,000 a year was passed; later, in 1883, the Great Eastern joined the lessees. The working and rental of the Whitechapel Junction undertaking was covered by agreement of 14 July 1884. The minimum sum paid only covered the first and second debentures, beyond that there was a Class B second charge debenture and a third and fourth, the needs of which in gross annual receipts totalled £361,122. With debentures issued to the tune of over £2¼ million, it is not surprising that the ordinary shareholders, of £3¼ million, never received a penny in the way of dividends. It was hoped that the lease and the running of through trains from the Circle would put all in a satisfactory state. Trains ran from various District destinations to what is now New Cross Gate and from the Metropolitan & Great Western to the SE station at New Cross. Some of these began or ended at Richmond, reached via the junction at The Grove, Hammersmith, and Turnham Green. Although a few Metropolitan trains ran through from Richmond to New Cross, Great Western trains did not run east of Aldgate until the Hammersmith & City electric multiple unit joint stock began running to Whitechapel and, after 1914, on to East London.

These through services from the Underground began on 6 October 1884; some days previously the South Eastern service (Addiscombe–Liverpool Street) ceased. The Great Eastern Railway provided a service from Liverpool Street on to the East London now partly in replacement of the trains the Railway & Canal Commission had thought so desirable from Liverpool Street to Brighton and which the Brighton company thought unremunerative. Some of these Great Eastern trains were projected beyond New Cross to East Croydon. No Brighton trains visited Liverpool Street after 1885, at least on regular business. The through trains from the Underground ceased on the electrification of the District (1 August 1905) and of the Metropolitan and Hammersmith & City (3 December 1906) and local steam services were provided to fill in the four trains an hour so withdrawn. A curious feature of the East London was the number of two-track stations at which trains turned back, involving running round the train in steam days and use of two cross-overs. By 1910 the Great Eastern service on the East London had come down to 7 journeys from Liverpool Street to East Croydon and 6 all the way back. The first from East Croydon turned back at Shoreditch. At that time there were 16 journeys from Liverpool Street to New Cross (LBSC) (now New Cross Gate), 16 journeys from Shoreditch to Peckham Rye on the Brighton's South London Line and a roughly 20-minute headway on the South Eastern service from Whitechapel to New Cross (South Eastern).

Great changes took place in the following year, when the chairman of the East London company, Lord Claud Hamilton, was pressing the urgency of electrification on the shareholders. A little modernisation was brought in by renaming Deptford Road station in July 1911 'Surrey Docks' and on 30 June the train services were modified at the instance of the LBSCR, which was providing improved services on the South London line and via Peckham Rye to Tulse Hill and Crystal Palace, by electrification, and contemplated electrifying the original London & Croydon route. The LBSCR service over the ELR from Shoreditch to Peckham Rye was withdrawn from 1 June 1911 because of the obstruction caused by terminating trains at Peckham Rye, and seven paths between New Cross and Croydon occupied by the Great Eastern trains were given up on 30 June.

Electrification of the East London was as joint an operation as its lease; the Great Eastern provided the £90,000 capital required, the Metropolitan District power from Lots Road, the Metropolitan the rolling stock and the South Eastern & Chatham chief engineer supervised the work. Last steam services ran on 30 March; Metropolitan electric trains began on 31 March 1913; eight an hour ran from Shoreditch to the two New Cross stations and four an hour from South Kensington to the New Cross termini which thus had half-hourly through services from the north side of the Circle. Early in 1914 the through service was modified by diversion to Hammersmith and yet another railway participated, as Great Western and Metropolitan Joint stock was used for the through working, which ended after traffic on 5 October 1941. Although counted as part of the Metropolitan Line on London Transport route diagrams the rolling stock for many years was ex-District and is now drawn from four-car 1938 Bakerloo sets. The East London Railway was purchased by the Southern Railway Company in 1925, to prevent its use as a jumping-off point for the Underground group in South-East London. The Whitechapel Junction debentures were purchased separately. Under nationalisation the East London was transferred to the London Transport Executive. The connections with British Railways have been severed at East London Junction (17 April 1966) and at New Cross.

The Croydon service of the Great Eastern was only one of several instances of non-radial routes kept open by that company. For that matter it pursued for many years provision of various facilities to the docks by alternative routes. This resulted from the early interest of the Eastern Counties & Thames Junction Railway which built a branch from Stratford to first the Lea at Canning Town in 1846 and then extended as the North Woolwich Railway to the Thames at North Woolwich on 14 June 1847. This was the same day as the curve from Stratford Western Junction to the North Woolwich line was opened for traffic; the Eastern Junction curve at Stratford was probably about the same date, as well as the curve from Chobham Farm Junction to Southern Junction. These branches were given a connection from Stratford to Victoria Park (Hackney Wick Junction) on the North London on 15 August 1854 via Central Junction and Fork Junction at Stratford. A service of North London trains to Stratford Bridge began on 16 October 1854, making a link between the LNW and Great Eastern systems. The NL service was withdrawn in the week ending 1 November 1866 and after that the Stratford Bridge–Victoria Park service was maintained in alternate years by the Great Eastern and North London companies until 1 November 1874. On 1 July 1873 the name Canning Town was adopted for what had previously been Barking Road; the station was resited on the north side of the road in 1888 and a bay for Victoria Park trains was added in 1895, when the service settled down as Canning Town–Victoria Park with Great Eastern trains. Stratford Bridge was renamed Stratford Market on 1 November 1880. From 1898 to 1923 it carried the suffix '(West Ham)'. The first station at Victoria Park on the North London was opened to general traffic on 14 June 1856, after a special opening for peace celebrations in Victoria Park on 29 May. A new station with platforms for the connecting trains from Stratford on the bifurcating line, giving cross-platform interchange for the Stratford–Poplar direction, came into service on 1 March 1866. The platform not required by Canning Town–Victoria Park trains, on the eastbound track, was removed 15 August 1895. The remaining platform on the Stratford line was closed on 1 November 1942 and the whole station on 8 November 1943.

The Tottenham & Hampstead Junction Railway, which in 1902 became joint Great Eastern and Midland property, was an example of unbounded optimism in that it was planned to join the London & North

Western's Hampstead Junction Railway at Gospel Oak to the Great Eastern, ignoring the fact that the LNWR already owned two-thirds of the capital of the North London which provided a perfectly adequate connection between the two systems. A service from Highgate Road to Fenchurch Street, operated by Great Eastern trains, began on 21 July 1868 and lasted to 30 January 1870; the circuitous route and the sparse population of the area between Seven Sisters and Holloway worked against its success. Once again an 'outer circle' type of route was rejected by the public.

By this time the Midland Railway was feeling its feet in London and so, instead of a train service via Stratford and Lea Bridge, the Tottenham & Hampstead line received trains over a connection from Kentish Town, opened for freight on 3 January 1870, and for passengers from Moorgate Street (Metropolitan) to Crouch Hill on 1 October 1870. This was extended on 1 May 1871 to South Tottenham. In the meantime the Great Eastern began main-line connections from its Cambridge service on 1 July 1870 (six up and five down) to what it called its 'West End terminus' – St Pancras. The station at Gospel Oak of the T & H had not been completed and in 1870 it was removed.

A platform alongside the Hampstead Junction station at Gospel Oak was again built in 1887 and a Great Eastern service begun on 1 August 1885 from Chingford to Highgate Road was extended to Gospel Oak on 4 June 1888. The junction at Gospel Oak was connected from the beginning of 1916, closed in 1920 and removed in September 1922; it was re-established on 11 March 1940 and was used extensively in the Second World War.

Soon after Epping Forest was acquired by the City of London Corporation it became a very popular resort, especially at weekends and Bank Holidays, but the Great Eastern persisted in feeling it had a duty to the residents of the northern suburbs, in making a connection between Hampstead Heath and Chingford. In 1910 there were seven journeys every weekday from Gospel Oak to Chingford, three extra on Saturdays and two which did not run on Saturdays, plus one Saturday trip from Gospel Oak to Wood Street, Walthamstow, only. The Sunday service consisted of seven trains. The $8\frac{1}{2}$-mile circuit of the periphery of the north-eastern suburbs occupied 25 or 26 minutes, and the services were increased in the summer months.

The Midland service from St Pancras to South Tottenham was extended over the Tottenham & Forest Gate Railway (a joint Midland and London, Tilbury & Southend venture) on 9 July 1894 to Wanstead Park and round the triangle by Little Ilford to a bay platform at East

Ham, but some of the service ran either to Barking (hence Gilly Potter's radio crack about the Rector of St Pancras and all stations to Barking) or Southend. In anticipation of such a service by the L T & S route the Great Eastern ran trains from Gospel Oak via Stratford to Southend in 1891 on summer Sundays, but in the summer of 1895 it became a daily service.

Other cross-country services in the Great Eastern suburban area included early endeavours to serve the Palace Gates branch (a name in itself designed to lure the ignorant into going by Great Eastern train to near the Alexandra Palace). The branch opened from Seven Sisters to Green Lanes (later Noel Park and Wood Green) on 1 January 1878 and was extended to Palace Gates on 7 October 1878; this was part of the suburban complex added to the Great Eastern system in the early 1870s along with the opening of the company's new City terminus at Liverpool Street. A spur from Seven Sisters to South Tottenham was completed on 1 January 1880 and enabled a service to run from Seven Sisters to Stratford. The same day the Great Eastern found a circuitous service from Palace Gates via Stratford to Fenchurch Street irresistible, but it lasted only to 31 August of that year. The next day it was diverted via the recently completed Salmon's Lane curve at Stepney to Blackwall, still thought to be a mecca for users of Thames steamers. The winter killed this service off and it last ran on 28 February 1881.

It was some years before another variant was tried. A Palace Gates to North Woolwich service began on 1 June 1887. Trains to the Palace Gates branch (which was not included in the Great Eastern electrification scheme) ended on 7 January 1963 for passengers and on 7 February 1965 for all traffic.

Other Great Eastern services that did not penetrate into the residential suburbs were Fenchurch Street to Blackwall, the original line of the London & Blackwall Railway, operated by the GER by three 2–4–0 tank engines (designed as 0–6–0T, but with the front section of coupling rod removed) operated by steam, after the cable traction phase, from April 1849 to 3 May 1926, when it ceased owing to the General Strike. It had been intended to withdraw the close headway train service in June 1926, because of tram and bus competition and the fact that shipping clerks no longer had to make personal visits to the docks with the growing use of the telephone. With the Blackwall line went the PLA's Millwall Extension Railway, originally a line divided between two dock companies and the GER between Millwall Junction and North Greenwich. The business on this line had been sapped by parallel bus services down each side of the Isle of Dogs and the aged Manning Wardle

2–4–0 tanks, which in dock company days sported Pears Soap advertisements, and the trains of two ancient Great Eastern oil-lit four-wheeled coaches had at last been replaced by former Great Western steam railcars in 1922.

The Port of London Authority did not reveal itself as expert in railway management because after the railcars had been purchased there was a delay before they could be put to work while new locking bars were provided at facing points. It had seemingly been overlooked that the long-wheelbase GW vehicles would not hold the original locking bars while they were traversing a turnout.

This line opened for freight to Millwall Docks on 18 December 1871 and for passenger traffic to North Greenwich on 29 July 1872. The first 5 chains from Millwall Junction were Great Eastern property; followed 41 chains first owned by the East & West India Dock Company and then acquired by the London & India Dock Company. At South Dock station were situated 11 chains from Millwall Junction, the offices of the joint committee responsible for this microcosm of railway and a passing loop. The swing bridges on this part of the line were the reason for the motive power being kept so light and in fact until 1880 it was confined to horse traction. Either side of South Dock there were 52 chains of line owned by the Millwall Dock Company in which the track rose to viaduct on which Millwall Dock Station, 72 chains from the start, was built. From here to North Greenwich, or North Greenwich and Cubitt Town as it was sometimes known, on 31 chains of Great Eastern territory, the Great Eastern at one time provided a locomotive, none other than *Ariel's Girdle* of 1851, much rebuilt. The best remembered engines were the tiny 2–4–0 tanks of the London & India Company and later the PLA, built in 1880. A curious feature of the Millwall Extension was that the last trains for passengers at South Dock stopped there at 6.29 p.m. and that after that the 15-minute service became half-hourly. Except for the traditional church interval on Sunday mornings there was a half-hourly Sunday service, although after October 1908 there were no connecting trains on the London & Blackwall line.

There were three services from the City to the Royal Docks area. On 14 June 1847 the spur at Stratford was opened that made possible the North Woolwich–Bishopsgate service that was on 2 February 1874 extended to Liverpool Street. At first the attraction of down-river steamer trips was so great that a platform at Bishopsgate was reserved for Woolwich line trains. Alternative facilities to Fenchurch Street became possible after 2 April 1849, but the Great Eastern and London & Blackwall companies were not at that time on more than rather frigid exchange-of-passengers terms at the interchange point. Through trains from North Woolwich to Fenchurch Street began on 1 June 1854. These ran via Stratford Bridge; Bow Road station on this route was added in 1876. The short cut for Woolwich trains, over the LTS line through Bromley, became possible with the opening of the curve from Abbey Mills Upper to Lower Junction and Great Eastern passenger trains from Fenchurch by this route began on 1 June 1858.

In 1910 there were 30 trains from Fenchurch Street via Bow Road and Stratford Market, 16 via Bromley (not all of which called at that station) in the middle of the day and 17 from Liverpool Street via Stratford Market. The branches from Custom House to Beckton (built by the Gas Light & Coke Company) and to Gallions (built by the Albert Dock Company) were opened to passenger service on 18 March 1874 and 3 August 1880 respectively. The Beckton branch opened for freight on 14 October 1872 and for the Gas Company's workmen's trains on 17 March 1873. The Dock Company had opened to Gallions for freight on 14 October 1878; it operated Allen-type locomotives purchased second-hand from the LNWR until 1896, when it handed over running to the GER. Whereas Beckton had a service of five trains a day to and from Stratford Market, the Gallions branch had two trains an hour to Fenchurch Street. Gallions closed for passengers on 8 September 1940 and altogether on 17 April 1966. Passenger trains to Beckton ceased on 29 December 1940; complete closure took place on 22 February 1971. The vestigial section of the L T & S service from Liverpool Street to Southend remained as eight or nine trains from Liverpool Street to Barking which left the Great Eastern main line after Forest Gate. It was a casualty of the First World War, as late as 1 May 1918, much later than most wartime withdrawals.

In the heyday of London rail connections there were many other short linking services, some with elaborate arrangements for their operation. The North London built a spur from Bow to the London, Tilbury & Southend at Bromley Junction, for example, opened on 18 May 1869. Two platforms were built on the diverging tracks at Bow and normally from 1871 to 1915 there was a half-hourly train service from Bow to Plaistow (LTS) calling at Bromley, very occasionally at West Ham after that station was built and terminating in a bay at Plaistow. A run-round loop for these trains was provided immediately north of the junction at Bow of the spur with the main line. The spur now lies under the concrete of a housing estate.

Two hopelessly circuitous L C & D branches ran from Nunhead, one to Greenwich Park, after 1 October 1888, but cut short for some years at Blackheath Hill, which was reached on 18 September 1871 and the other to Crystal Palace (High Level). This one was built by the Crystal Palace & South London Junction Railway, opened on 1 August 1865 and inclined at 1 in 78 most of its picturesque but unremunerative way. So in the First World War it was closed from 1 January 1917 to 1 March 1919 and in the Second World War from 22 May 1944 to 4 March 1946. It was a favourite route for theorists to suggest as a means of getting the Bakerloo tube into the south-eastern suburbs, but it was finally closed on 20 September 1954 and replaced by a 20-minute headway bus service. It has since been built over at various points. The Greenwich Park branch succumbed on 1 January 1917; after that a berthed coaching set that had been insecurely braked ran down from Nunhead into the tunnel beyond Blackheath Hill and was not located for some time, since rumour had it that a fortnight elapsed before anybody even looked for it. The bridge over the South Eastern at St John's was removed and since then the line has been built over as well as the alignment being further interrupted by demolition of the bridge over Brookmill Road. The Lewisham loops in 1929 made a use of the first section of the line from Nunhead as a through route.

CRYSTAL PALACE and BECKENHAM JUNCTION (Steam Car—One class only).
South Eastern and Chatham.

Miles		Week Days.										
		mrn	mrn	aft	aft	aft	aft	aft	aft	aft	aft	aft
	Crystal Palace...........................dep.	1018	1142	1257	3 38	4 25	5 52	6 52	8 22	9 40	1030	11 2
3	Beckenham Junction 244, 270, 272...arr.	1026	1150	1 5	3 49	4 33	6 0	7 1	8 30	9 49	1038	1111

Miles		Week Days.										
		mrn	mrn	aft	aft	aft	Sats.	aft	aft	aft	aft	aft	aft
	Beckenham Junction................dep.	9 58	11 0	1240	2 40	4 e 5		4 8	5 0	6 26	7 28	9 20	9 58	1043
3	Crystal Palace *.....................arr.	10 8	1110	1250	2 50	4e15		4 18	5 10	6 36	7 38	9 30	10 8	1055

e Except Saturdays.   * Low Level Station, nearly ¾ mile to High Level Station.

Timetable 2. Crystal Palace and Beckenham Junction (Steam Car—One class only)
(South Eastern & Chatham)

The services maintained by the L C & D and the South Eastern & Chatham companies from Beckenham Junction to Crystal Palace and Beckenham Junction to Norwood Junction were reminders of the L C & D original approach to London over the West End of London & Crystal Palace (Farnborough Extension) Railway, local service on which began on 3 May 1858. Through L C & D services to London dated from 3 December 1860, but the L C & D had its own route via Herne Hill to Victoria from 1 July 1863. The trains over the curve between Spur Junction and Norwood Junction began on 18 June 1862. In 1910 the 2½-mile Beckenham Junction–Norwood Junction service had 8 trips one way and 9 the other. The steam railcar ran 11 trips from Crystal Palace to Beckenham Junction with one extra on Saturdays the other way. Judging by the train times – first departure from Beckenham

Junction 9.58 a.m. – these links were definitely not intended for commuters. Both these short services disappeared in the 1914–18 war, but the Crystal Palace–Beckenham Junction connection was restored on 3 March 1929 with the third rail electrification of the Brighton system. Since 1 December 1915 quite sizeable trees had grown in the roadbed.

The connections which have been broken over the years have not been missed greatly by the public. The dense network of bus services partly accounts for this, but still more the growing use of the private car for any journey not precisely covered by public transport seems to make unnecessary provision of public transport over any routes except those needed by large numbers of users.

three

METROPOLITAN
DISTRICT OUTER
CIRCLE

It is difficult to say when the idea of an Outer Circle railway round London seized the imagination of railway promoters. For some years into the railway era there was a complete lack of communication between railways south and north of the Thames and only such junctions between groups of lines going in the same direction as had been enforced by Parliament. The doyen of London railways, the London & Greenwich, thus became the only railway entry permitted from the south to the London area and its London Bridge terminus, officially opened on 14 December 1836, became also the terminus for the London & Croydon (opened from what is now West Croydon to Corbett's Lane Junction with the London & Greenwich on 5 June 1839), the London & Brighton (opened from Haywards Heath to Jolly Sailor, Norwood Junction, on the London & Croydon on 12 July 1841) and the South Eastern (opened from Tonbridge to Redhill on the London & Brighton on 26 May 1842). As an additional complication, jointly-owned lines not having been established as a practical feature of railway management, a moiety of the London & Brighton between Norwood and Redhill was transferred to the South Eastern. That company had in any event originally planned to build a more direct route from Norwood to Edenbridge *en route* to Tonbridge.

This southern aspect of railways was not repeated anywhere else round London. On the north-west, looking at the map, one can give credence to the idea that the Great Western route into the Metropolis was originally intended to join that of the London & Birmingham on its way from Willesden to Camden, but such a plan was effectively prevented by Brunel's decision to adopt the 7 ft gauge in place of the 4 ft 8½ in. to which the London & Birmingham was committed.

So main lines came into London to London Bridge in 1836, to Euston (London & Birmingham) in 1837, to Nine Elms (London & South Western, originally London–Southampton) 1838, Paddington (Great Western) 1838, and Shoreditch (Eastern Counties) 1839. For reasons of expediency rather than the dictates of the legislature, the Eastern Counties line was joined at Stratford in 1840 by the Northern & Eastern Railway. Both these lines adopted the 5 ft gauge at first through Braithwaite, the Eastern Counties engineer, having been not so much impressed by Brunel's arguments for the 7 ft gauge as fearful that he might prevail, though what help being 3½ in. wider would have been, had it been decided to expand to 7 ft instead of contracting to 4 ft 8½ in. (as was eventually done by these two railways on two days in the autumn of 1844) is hard to imagine.

Next railway into London was another approximately 5 ft gauge line (5 ft 1 in. to be precise), the London & Blackwall, designed to be a City railway and so cable operated. Two winding engines were provided, at Minories and Poplar; from the latter point to Blackwall trains operated by momentum from the opening day, 6 July 1840. From Minories operation was similarly by momentum after 2 August 1841, when the line was extended to a terminus at Fenchurch Street, actually inside the boundaries of the City of London. This railway, second urban system in the world, had all the characteristics of a rapid transit route, with most of its roadbed elevated on viaduct, highly cost-intensive, in order to avoid interrupting traffic in the numerous streets crossed, and with a specialised traction system. After numerous failures which were not eliminated by substitution of wire rope for hemp, steam traction was adopted with the standard 4 ft 8½ in. gauge on 15 February 1849. This opened the way for the Blackwall Extension Railway to join Stepney on the London & Blackwall with Bow on the Eastern Counties from 2 April 1849. But relations between the two undertakings were not cordial and if the junction was made it was not used. H. V. Borley, in a letter to the July 1974 issue of the *Journal of the Railway and Canal Historical Society*, suggests that certain trains on the Blackwall Extension exchanged passengers with the Eastern Counties at what that company called Victoria Park and Bow, but the Blackwall company named as Bow and Bromley. Although the Extension line service interval was given as 15 minutes, it appears that the service to the exchange platforms, regulated by the number of connections the Eastern Counties was prepared to make, was sparse. The original station at Bow Road, a typical road-level booking hall under viaduct platforms, was visible early in the twentieth century on the south side of that thoroughfare and for a time was in use as a 'fleapit' cheap 'electric theatre' showing low-quality films, and at another time as auction rooms, any use being restricted by the cramped proportions of the original structure.

[31]

The first railway to set out to join other railways in the London area was established at the East & West India Docks & Birmingham Junction Railway and was intended in 1846 to join the London & Birmingham system to the docks, connecting it (when the London & Birmingham had become part of the London & North Western) at Camden with the dock system at Poplar. The more succinct title of North London Railway was taken from 1 January 1853. In the first instance it was opened from the neighbourhood of south of Highbury (later Islington) to Bow Common on the Blackwall Extension where the junction point became known as Gas Factory Junction and was situated at the top of a curving bank over ¼ mile long, mainly at 1 in 99, which took North London trains from the cutting below Bow Road to the Blackwall Company's viaduct. The signal box at Gas Factory Junction was for many years staffed by the North London Railway. Train service from Islington to Fenchurch Street, the Blackwall Company's terminus, began on 26 September 1850 at 15-minute intervals. Although the London & Blackwall Railway promptly withdrew its service to the Bow & Bromley exchange platforms, the Eastern Counties connecting trains continued to call for the next three months until early in 1851. As the junction with the London & North Western at Camden was not available until the first half of 1851 it seems likely that the early North London train service was maintained by London & Blackwall locomotives. To late-twentieth-century eyes it seems roundabout in the extreme, but fast passage from the Camden Town area to the City, with the last stops at Bow and Stepney, appeared most attractive and the traffic was an unexpected bonus to investors in the North London Railway; two-thirds of the shares were in any event in the possession of the London & North Western Railway company.

Next, in 1853, came the North & South Western Junction Railway, intended to link the London & South Western Railway at Brentford with the London & North Western near what became Willesden Junction. It was authorised on 24 July 1851 between a point at or near the London & North Western Railway station at Willesden and the Windsor, Staines and South Western line loop of the London & South Western Railway between Feltham and Barnes, and at what became known as Old Kew Junction near Brentford and came into operation for London & South Western Railway freight trains on 15 February 1853, and for a North London passenger service which ran from 1 August 1853, operating from Fenchurch Street. The North London's original objective of joining freight access to East and West India Docks was achieved by the opening of the line from Bow Junction to Poplar on 1

January 1852. When coal from Midland fields did not yet come to London mainly by rail, the North London had an import traffic from the docks in coal conducted to suburban stations by the Northumberland and Durham Coal Company with its own locomotives and wagons in the style of the original toll-road concept of the railway; the company paid £10,000 a year for the privilege but had to be bought out in 1859 owing to the impracticability of working a steam railway thus. In the early days the North London owned its own coaches and according to George Bolland Newton, general manager from 1877 to 1900, they were built of papier mâché, showing that the plastic age is already over a century old. Motive power came from London & Blackwall engines at first and then for a time from the London and North Western Railway.

The important thing is that the North London route round the perimeter of the built-up area of North-East London attracted 97,000 passengers in the first month; and 186,775 by January 1851. This refocused the attention of both speculators and authorities on the possibilities of 'outer circle' projects, especially when the success of the even more roundabout North & South Western Junction route was taken into account. Parliament in 1863 and 1864 was appalled at the volume of railway proposals for London, inspired partly by the success of local undertakings and especially the North London, and accelerated after 1863 by the success of the Metropolitan, the world's first underground, the first part of which had been opened on 10 January 1863. According to Charles E. Lee there were 259 London projects in the session of 1864, the mileage of which would have totalled some 300. *Bradshaw's Railway Manual* for 1864 records 69 Parliamentary Bills for railways promoted in the 35-mile radius of the Metropolis and 5 more noted which had fallen through in consequence of no Bill having been deposited by 23 December 1863.

The railway situation in the centre of London arose to a large extent from the decisions of the Royal Commission on Railway Termini within or in the Immediate Vicinity of the Metropolis set up in April 1846 when, as a result of the railway mania, there seemed some danger of the centre of London being overrun by various railway schemes. Caring more for the absence of disturbance to the existing population and perhaps still more for property, the Royal Commission decided to minimise railway mileage in the centre of London and considered that the advantages to through passengers to be obtained from extension of existing lines into the heart of London were much exaggerated and, for the sake of short-distance passengers, such plans were quite unjustifiable. The report was issued quite quickly, on 27 June 1846; expense and disturbance to property were the main objections to urban railway construction, and at a time when the commercial railway was a relative novelty (only a decade and a half old) and the use of the main lines for suburban traffic was practically unknown it is not surprising that the idea of a central station used by a multiplicity of railway companies was refuted. Alarmist views of the dangerous railway operating problems that would arise in such a station before the universal introduction of signal boxes and the invention of interlocking (which did not get off the ground until 1852) prevailed, and the possible congestion of street traffic arising from such a concentration of railway services, at a time when many schemes of improvement had been mooted and few carried out, was also a deterrent. Another damper on the authorising of any of the fifteen projects north of the Thames and the four on the south bank that were considered was the Admiralty reaction to further bridges over the river; their obstructive attitude was echoed by the Royal Commission.

Farringdon Street was at this time a popular area for a terminal because the City had plans for reconstruction in the Fleet Valley. The Eastern Counties had a proposal for a Farringdon Street terminal, with a new approach from Tottenham on the Northern & Eastern branch. But both George Hudson, at that time chairman of the Eastern Counties, and Carr Glyn, chairman of the London & Birmingham, gave their support to the condemnation of a central terminus which would be used by several railways. The London & Birmingham had contemplated extension to the Farringdon area but was appalled at the cost estimates. Instead they wanted the provision of their subsidiary, which ultimately took shape as the North London, from the neighbourhood of Camden to the Docks. Other north side plans were only partially formulated and two that reached the Bill stage failed to pass Parliamentary Standing Orders. The Royal Commissioners were in favour of two schemes only: a belt round the north of London and an embankment on the north bank of the river incorporating provision of a local railway.

South of the Thames plans were more advanced. The London & South Western extension to Waterloo had been authorised in 1845 and now it was desired to go on to a site that the London County Council trams years later described as 'Hop Exchange', on the west side of London Bridge. In fact it reached Waterloo in 1848. The South Eastern wanted to cross the same area with a line off the Bricklayers' Arms branch to Hungerford Bridge, as did the then independent North Kent Railway with a terminus at Union Street, also on the west of the London Bridge south side approach. As this Bill was rejected and eventually

[34]

revived in different form for a South Eastern subsidiary it did not influence matters; although the Royal Commission favoured the Union Street terminal site but also backed the South Eastern extension, provided it was revised and level crossings both of streets and the London South Western extension eliminated. A line to join routes on the south of London with those to the north but outside the area under investigation was a pious hope which took the best part of two decades to be arrived at. In the upshot Parliament sanctioned the North London route from Camden to Poplar and the London South Western Railway London Bridge extension.

What was important was the freezing of the termini more or less upon the irregular oval ring of the boundaries laid down by the Royal Commission, from Vauxhall Bridge Road by way of Grosvenor Place, Park Lane, and Edgware Road on the west side, Marylebone, Euston and City Roads on the north, Bishopsgate Street, London Bridge and Borough High Street on the east, and Borough Road, Lambeth Road and Vauxhall Bridge on the south, varied practically for terminal purposes as the south bank of the Thames.

At this time suburban traffic, until the expansion of the 1870s 'and the introduction of workmen's trains' at cheap fares (voluntarily on the Metropolitan and statutorily on the London, Chatham & Dover) extensions into the Metropolis, ostensibly because of their destruction of property, had little importance either to railways or public, and the majority of workers lived either close to their places of work or were prepared to walk quite considerable distances each day. As late as the 1930s I had dealings with a printer who saw nothing remarkable in walking to and fro each day at the age of over 65 between Denmark Hill and Blackfriars Road. The habit of pedestrianism was ingrained among a wide cross-section of the public; from 1867 to 1887 my grandfather walked often when staying at his father-in-law's country cottage in Leytonstone to a shop near Aldgate and thought nothing of doing so before opening the shop at 0800 and, after closing it, returning 12 hours later. On one occasion only it was the family tradition that he had lingered on the way, to pick up golden sovereigns dropping from the tailboard of a hay cart *en route* from an Essex farm to Whitechapel Haymarket. More about the development of suburban railway traffic and workmen's fares will be found in Charles E. Lee's *Passenger Class Distinctions*.

Facilities, as always, did beget traffic, but the development of the local travel habit, and especially of the process of commuting, was slow, although aided by the regular headways of the train services to

Greenwich and Croydon and then by short branches with train services convenient for the purpose of working in the central area to such places as Richmond, Loughton and Beckenham in the 1840s and 1850s. The big expansion took place with what might be described as the London railway mania of the 1860s, sparked off by the promotion, completion and opening of the Metropolitan Railway, the world's first urban underground line. Charles Pearson, the City of London Solicitor from 1839 onwards, embraced a good many causes, among them the germ of the idea of garden suburbs with cheap train connections, the central city terminus scheme for joint railway use and a scheme for covered railway links, coupled with road improvements and other refinements of town planning, including walkways, arcades and shopping precincts. These materialised as a project for a City Terminus Company, to be joined by the Bayswater, Paddington and Holborn Bridge Railway with an underground approach, whose scheme one can discern most of the north side of the Inner Circle. The Bayswater, Paddington & Holborn Bridge Company renamed their project North Metropolitan, withdrew to Edgware Road to stifle local opposition and, because they were mainly interested in local traffic along the New Road and to the City, shown by bus operators since 1832 to have the makings of a gold mine, they dropped the City Terminus project.

The lines laid down for the location of London termini by the Royal Commission in 1846 almost made it a certainty that the Metropolitan Railway, to which the name North Metropolitan was simplified in 1854, would seek to promote a line joining up the ring of main-line termini. Ten years later this seemed a most laudable objective to the House of Lords Select Committee on Metropolitan Communication, which declared that

> it would be desirable to complete an inner circuit of railway
> that should abut upon, if it did not actually join, nearly all
> the principal termini in the Metropolis, commencing with the
> extension in an easterly and southerly direction, of the
> Metropolitan from Finsbury Circus (Moorgate), at the one end,
> and in a westerly and southerly direction, from Paddington, at
> the other, and connecting the extremities of those lines by a
> line on the north side of the Thames; such a continuous line
> of railway would afford means of distributing the passenger
> traffic arriving by the main lines of railway, and also absorb a
> very large portion of the omnibus and cab traffic and thus
> essentially relieve the crowded streets.

By this time the ring of termini had in fact either materialised or existed as projects. The original Great Western terminus at Paddington of 1838 had given place to one with a frontage on Praed Street in 1854; the London & North Western's Euston (1837) still stood back from Euston Road; St Pancras had been planned by the Midland in 1862 and sanctioned by Act of the following year; King's Cross had opened in 1852; Broad Street, authorised in 1861, was to open to the public in 1865; Liverpool Street, mooted in one form or another for a number of years, appealed to the Select Committee of 1863 and was sanctioned, along with a new network of suburban routes, in 1864; Fenchurch Street had been in existence since 1840; London Bridge had the distinction of being the senior of the London termini, dating from 1836; the South Eastern Railway had reached the north bank of the river at Cannon Street in 1866 and Charing Cross, on the Hungerford Market site, two years previously; lastly Victoria, the outstanding case of a London terminus provided by a terminal company, the Victoria Station & Pimlico, catering for the London, Brighton & South Coast, London, Chatham & Dover and Great Western Railways had been open from 1860.

To define the area in which the 1863 Select Committee was making regulations, it was thought that the area specified by the Royal Commission of 1846 was too restricted. A new Metropolitan Railway District was defined to begin at Barking Road (renamed Canning Town in 1873) station of the Great Eastern North Woolwich branch and with a boundary running thence along the Great Eastern line to Lea Bridge station, from there in a straight line to Seven Sisters station on the Great Northern Railway (opened in 1861 and more familiar as Seven Sisters Road or as Finsbury Park, which was its new name in 1869), thence in another straight line to the eastern end of the Hampstead Tunnel of the Hampstead & City Junction (better known as the Hampstead Junction Railway), along that railway to its junction with the West London (at Willesden Junction), thence along that line (and the West London Extension) across the River Thames to a junction with the London, Chatham & Dover, along that railway to Brixton Road (now Brixton) station, in a straight line to Lewisham Junction on the Mid-Kent and then in a straight line across the River Thames to the north bank and back to Barking Road station. Unfortunately this area was also far too limited in size as it omitted a good many parts of the developing suburbia and even excluded a great many rival London area undertakings which were determined in their scope by the ordinary (and it must be confessed, haphazard) Parliamentary Bill procedure.

[37]

For example, west of the West London route there were proposals for the Finchley, Willesden & Acton Railway; the Hammersmith & City (Extensions) for a line to Kew and Richmond, the Kew, Turnham Green & Hammersmith; the London & South Western (Kensington, Hammersmith & Richmond New Lines); Hammersmith & Wimbledon; North & South Western Junction (extension to Kew and Richmond); Kingston, Tooting & London; and Tooting, Merton & Wimbledon Extension. These lines, criss-crossing the west and south-west areas of Greater London ripe for building development, no doubt were properly appraised by the respective Parliamentary committees, but they were not examined in the comprehensive sense of their effect on Metropolitan railway communications as a whole. The area round the Crystal Palace, to which attention began in the 1850s and was continuing in the 1860s, was also omitted from consideration. The lack of universal treatment of railway planning for the London area may be attributed to the trait of amateurism manifest in so much of British administration and emphasised in the naïve questioning of witnesses appearing before the Select Committee.

The principal points on which the Committee reported after enlarging the area of its interest as outlined above were seventeen in number. It was stated that:

Squares and open spaces in the Metropolis are not to be taken unnecessarily for the purposes of a railway.

It would be objectionable to allow the construction of a great central station in the Metropolis.

In the construction of any new lines of railway within the Metropolitan Railway District, subways, covered ways or tunnels appear preferable where circumstances admit of them.

With the view of giving further effect to the provisions in favour of the labouring classes contained in the 191st Standing Order it is desirable 'That in every Bill for making any work, in the construction of which compulsory power is given to take 30 or more houses inhabited by the labouring classes in any one parish or place, a Clause be inserted to enact that the company shall, not less than four weeks before taking any such houses, make known their intention to take the same either by personal notice to heads of families inhabiting the same, at the time of giving such notice or by placards, handbills, or other general notice placed in public view within a reasonable distance from such houses, and that the company shall not take any such houses until they have obtained the certificate of a Justice that it has been proved to his satisfaction that the company have made known their intention to take the same in manner required by this provision'.

That heavy traffic in goods and especially in minerals, could as a general rule be most conveniently carried from the railways lying north of the Thames, to the railways lying south of the Thames, by lines not passing through the central portions of the Metropolis.

This last was no doubt a dig at some previous Parliamentary Committee which as recently as 6 August 1860 had passed the Act for the London, Chatham & Dover Metropolitan Extension, railway number 2 of which was from Herne Hill, across the Thames at Blackfriars to the eastward side of Farringdon Street and provided for two junctions of 27 chains and 11 chains respectively in length, with the Metropolitan Railway. At the time of the 1863 report through traffic had not begun; the London, Chatham & Dover Railway and Widened Lines link did not enter service until 1 January 1866.

The Committee was in fact in favour of the East London Railway in some form or other; several schemes were included in the Bills lodged for 1864. The recommendation read 'that there should be a line of railway on the eastern side of the Metropolis connecting the railways north and south of the Thames'.

It was considered desirable that additional facilities should be afforded and less onerous arrangements in reference to tolls made for the passage by the railways on the western side of the Metropolis of minerals and goods traffic from some of the northern railways to the railways and district of country south of the Thames.

'Additional railway communication is needed in the densely populated part of the Metropolis,' ran the next clause, 'and it is desirable that railway communication, where it does not already exist, should be established between the various lines of railway.'

An exception to the ban on more central locations for main-line termini was to be made in the case of the Great Eastern, which as the Eastern Counties had established its temporary terminus at Devonshire Street, Mile End, in 1839 and had reached Shoreditch on 1 July 1840, still separated from the City of London boundary by the quarter-mile length of Norton Folgate, and deemed by many Victorians to be in a cut-throat neighbourhood. That view of its remoteness from the more elegant parts of the capital was not entirely eliminated by renaming the station Bishopsgate in 1846. Now it was declared that

> the Great Eastern should be allowed to establish a more central station than it has at present and be placed in communication with the lines running to the western part of the Metropolis.
>
> That it is not desirable to bring the main stations of any of the principal long lines of railway, except the Great Eastern, farther into London than is at present authorised, but that one or more railways should be made for carrying passengers from different parts of London to the main stations of the long lines. Such new lines not to be in the hands of any one of the present great companies, but placed under such management as to ensure equal advantages to all.

The positive recommendation for the Inner Circle followed in words already set out. It was further suggested that the line might be undertaken in connection with the construction by the municipal authorities of the City, or the Metropolitan Board of Works, of new streets urgently required in many of the crowded parts of the Metropolis. Under some of these new streets, and under a portion of the proposed Thames Embankment (north side) and under some of the existing wide thoroughfares, new lines of railway might be advantageously and economically constructed; and arrangements might be made by which railway companies might, in consideration of being allowed to construct their lines under the streets and the Thames Embankment without charge for the land, be willing to undertake the construction of other parts of the lines required for completing the circuit of communication, which, if constructed not in connection with such cheap lines, would be so expensive as to be unremunerative.

At this point the Outer Circle idea was praised, although its application was limited to the areas north of the Thames. 'It would be desirable', said the Select Committee, 'that an outer circle of railway should be formed within the Metropolitan Railway District, in its course intersecting and communicating with the principal lines of railway north of the River Thames. It might be convenient to bring this outer circle, at certain points, into communication with the inner circle.'

The Committee were of opinion that every such system of internal railway communication for the Metropolis should be under one management and they thought that this might be secured without interfering with the existing practice of allowing free competition in plans by providing through a Standing Order:

That in any notice for any Bill it should be stated that the Bill
may be so altered in its course through Parliament as to unite
the whole or some portions of such railway with some one or
other existing railways or work.

The suggestion that a commission be appointed to consider the building of railways in the Metropolis was thought to be too delaying and not
likely to solve the problem of the supply of capital.

The Committee hoped that if their general views were thought
satisfactory by the House, then means would be taken to render future
legislation conformable with its views. This could be done by appointing
a committee in future sessions to consider schemes coming into the
Metropolitan Railway District. A report from the Board of Trade on
such schemes would be desirable each session. The Metropolitan Board
of Works and the Commissioner of Sewers for the City should have the
plans and Bills for such schemes and if they thought fit they could report
on them. The two Houses should arrange that all Bills relating to
railways in the Metropolitan Railway District should be introduced in
one House, be grouped together and referred to the same Select Committee. This was a point made against the methods of all private Bill
legislation, that a committee of each House went over it, thus duplicating
the work and increasing the cost of obtaining an Act.

There was little urgency on the part of Parliament to adopt the views
of the Committee on Metropolitan Communication; except in name, the
Outer Circle scheme never got off the ground; physical completion of
the Great Eastern terminus took a decade and the Inner Circle scheme
a score of years; for the consolidation of London urban railway management, the world had to wait until 1933. One of the reasons for the early
delays was the financial panic of 1866, sparked off by the failure of the
merchant banking house of Overend, Gurney & Company on 'Black
Friday', 10 May 1866, and a resultant chain of bankruptcies, after which
Bank Rate stood at 10 per cent until 16 August. Another unexpected
obstacle was the divided management foreseen as harmful by the Committee which actually came about and proved more pernicious than
could reasonably have been predicted. This was brought about by the
method of financing the costly business of building the Inner Circle.

Having backed the circle railway idea the committee became uneasily
aware of the fact that it was beyond the capacity of the Metropolitan
company to raise all the money needed, and they therefore encouraged
formation of another concern, the Metropolitan District Railway, to
bear the burden of finding the capital needed for the southern side of

the circle. So in 1864 the joint committee of both Houses of Parliament authorised the Metropolitan Railway (Notting Hill & Brompton Extension) of 29 July by which the Metropolitan was to extend from a junction between Edgware Road and Praed Street via Paddington and High Street, Kensington, to South Kensington, and on the same day the Metropolitan Railway (Tower Hill Extension) Act for it to extend from Moorgate via Aldgate. The south side of the circle was to be built by the Metropolitan District Railway from South Kensington to Tower Hill via Victoria and a subway under the Thames Embankment. Embellishments to the circle included a connection from High Street to Earl's Court and on to the West London Railway near Addison Road, Kensington, on that line and secondly paralleling the Metropolitan line between South Kensington and Gloucester Road which went on to terminate with a station abutting on the West London Extension Railway at West Brompton.

This scheme had been outlined by John Fowler as a means of completing the Inner Circle and obtaining traffic from the London & North Western (via Addison Road) and the London & South Western and London, Brighton & South Coast companies (via West Brompton) to enlarge the Metropolitan District catchment area, it being feared (rightly) that Kensington would not produce enough traffic to pay interest on the huge capital required. The first link lay fallow for several years and the other never materialised at all. But in addition he prepared a plan for the Outer Circle scheme, which although welcomed in general terms by the Select Committee, they then included among the schemes which they rejected. They were probably right to do so, writing with hindsight over a century later, although it is attractive, as I said in the 1973 presidential address to the London Underground Railway Society, to think of the possible circumstances if Fowler's proposal had been carried out, of the loudspeakers at Clapham Junction announcing: 'The train standing at Platform 17 is a District Line Outer Circle train for Chelsea, High Street, Kilburn, Stamford Hill, Victoria Park, Bow, Limehouse and New Cross.'

The abortive Outer Circle project of the Metropolitan District company would have begun at the West London Extension platforms (now 16 and 17) at Clapham Junction and, throwing off a spur which would have cut a swathe through the housing site on the slopes of Lavender Hill in the direction of the link from the West London Extension to the London, Chatham & Dover Railway at Factory Junction, the Outer Circle would have left the West London Extension on the west. After passing under the Brighton and South Western tracks it

[42]

headed northward towards the west side of Battersea Park; paralleling the park it was planned to cross the Thames just west of where Albert Bridge was built in 1873. It would then have aimed at the District Railway's alignment just west of Gloucester Road and running parallel to the Metropolitan, and have formed the east side of the triangle that was built by the Metropolitan District Company without powers in 1870, the contentious Cromwell Curve that the District Company used for its part of the circle service for a short time in 1884 to improve its portion of the mileage for the trains concerned. From the District platforms at High Street Kensington the Outer Circle would have continued through the high ground of Campden Hill, presumably also in a real tunnel, to Notting Hill. Where the Inner Circle turns east towards Paddington the Outer Circle would have continued in a northerly direction in tunnel to cross the Hammersmith & City Railway and the Great Western main line about their point of divergence at Westbourne Park. Curves from the Hammersmith & City and the Great Western would have enabled trains from the London & South Western Railway eventually to have made a short cut on to the Outer Circle as well as traffic from the Great Western system and its connections. Turning as a surface railway north-north-east, the Outer Circle next aimed at Kilburn, London & North Western Railway, where curves were proposed west to north from the London & North Western Railway and south to east to the London & North Western Railway and its subsidiary, the North London. Maintaining its direction with a short tunnel under West End Lane the Outer Circle would have turned eastward just before crossing the Hampstead Junction Railway, putting out spurs towards the as yet unbuilt Midland main line in the Child's Hill direction and to Finchley Road & Frognal station of the Hampstead Junction. Adding another tunnel to the Belsize tunnels of the Midland and Hampstead Heath tunnel on the Hampstead Junction, it would have crossed that line just south of Gospel Oak and picked up a spur therefrom. In fact there may have been a thought in adopting this layout that the expense of tunnelling Haverstock Hill might have been avoided by using the Hampstead Junction tracks. From Gospel Oak the Outer Circle would have crossed the area which later became the Midland Kentish Town locomotive sheds and struck off for Finsbury Park on the Great Northern, or Seven Sisters Road as it was then known. A pair of spurs would have provided means for north-bound traffic from either segment of the circle to the Great Northern Railway.

Here the projected trace of the Outer Circle ran outside the boundary of the Metropolitan Railway District and crossed the alignment of the new Great Eastern route to Enfield just north of the site of its Stoke Newington station, before curving south-eastward to cross the Hackney Downs–Tottenham main-line link of the Great Eastern suburban projects about the site of its Clapton station. It now ran on higher ground above the Lea Valley to come alongside the North London Dalston–Poplar line when it was turning south at Victoria Park. Connections were intended to the North London, for East and West India Docks and to the Great Eastern Victoria Park–Stratford branch for the Royal group of docks. Crossing the North London about Old Ford it would have passed over the Great Eastern main line just east of Coborn Road station, and spurs would have made connection with the Great Eastern in the Victoria Park–Liverpool Street and New Cross–Stratford directions. Crossing the London & Blackwall Extension Railway close to Gas Factory Junction yet another link to the North London Railway was proposed – so that northbound traffic on the Outer Circle could turn back towards Poplar and the East and West India Docks.

The Outer Circle was here to turn towards Regent's Canal Dock, which it left to the west, and rose to the bridge demanded by the Admiralty for crossing the Thames in the days of tall ships, 130 ft above the Thames and of 750 ft span, at Limehouse. This would have landed it on the south bank very much among the Surrey Commercial Docks, an area from which the Outer Circle made a beeline for the point at which the Surrey Canal passed under the Brighton and South Eastern Railways. A flying junction was projected with the London, Brighton & South Coast Railway main line, a spur to the projected Old Kent Road and Peckham Rye (South London) line of the London, Brighton & South Coast Railway and a spur to the South Eastern North Kent line.

From the neighbourhood of New Cross to the complex on the east of Clapham Junction even the optimists behind the Metropolitan District Outer Circle scheme shrank from offering to duplicate the South London line which had already been authorised to the Brighton company as far as Brixton (30 June 1862) and was to be completed by the London, Chatham & Dover (Act of 14 July 1864), the respective openings being 13 August 1866 and 1 May 1867.

Although the 1864 Select Committee liked the idea of an Outer Circle the detail of the Metropolitan District scheme was rejected; the Board of Trade had had two broadsides on the subject from James Cawkwell, general manager of the London & North Western Railway, first on 13 January 1864 and then on 26 January. He was particularly anxious to protect the traffic and potential traffic of the London & North Western Railway protégé, the North London, and to safeguard the London &

[44]

North Western Company's interest in the West London and West London Extension Railways, and contended that existing authorised schemes nearly covered the ground. Evidence was given to the committee by E. Stewart, the secretary of the London & North Western Company, who said: 'I do not believe the circular railways will be attended with any practical convenience to the public.' In this he touched the vital fact that passengers will not go by a time-consuming and costly roundabout route without resenting the necessity of doing so. The use of alternative means of going from Paddington to Victoria or vice versa, such as bus route 36 (established on this route by motor buses for over 60 years) or the various underground and tube railway links, and also between Victoria and King's Cross, vindicates this view over a century later as has the comparatively limited use made of the costly eastern section of the Inner Circle where means of shortening the route nearly prevailed while it was still under construction.

So it is probable that attractive though aspects of the Outer Circle scheme might be, Londoners have not lost a lot through failure to implement the idea. Cawkwell was quick to point out that freight connections to do practically all that the Outer Circle claimed in linking the many main lines radiating from London existed or were planned in the early 1860s and, in using lines wholly or partly in the hands of the companies requiring the freight service links, would be less costly to operate and require less co-ordinated action than the use of the Metropolitan District Company's Outer Circle. For over a century there have been sound practical reasons for not raising the capital or destroying the band of houses round the Metropolis that would have been required to carry out the Outer Circle scheme.

four

WHAT MIGHT HAVE BEEN

The special case of the Metropolitan District's Outer Circle railway has always appealed to the writer as an example of a railway which had theoretical merit that steadily diminished as its features were more closely examined. It is only one of an extremely large number of London railway proposals which have been rejected by Parliament or by investors and which have come to nothing in the end. In comparatively few of these cases can one feel that the Londoner has been the loser.

There is such a multiplicity of schemes that one cannot hope to describe them all but they are susceptible of some degree of classification. The peripheral theme has been a recurrent one; the circular railway attracts both promoters expecting traffic from links between main lines, and theorists who deem such a link-up desirable. Radial routes attracted those eager to fill gaps between territory served by main lines; internal London area routes were designed prolifically in the days of the horse bus, first as viaduct railways, then as shallow undergrounds and particularly in the deep-level tube railway boom; then the grim facts of motor bus competition brought a long pause in respect of new major routes promoted in Parliament until the recent Victoria Line crystallised with the new ideals of shallow curves and wide station spacing.

Two lines in the internal railway category were rejected at once by the 1864 Committee. They were both short and intended for pneumatic operation, with the carriage or carriages of the train blown through a tube by air pressure; the system was devised by the unfortunate Thomas Webster Rammell. The facts about his work from 1857 on goods and letter-carrying railways, promoted after 1859 by the Pneumatic Dispatch Co. Ltd, among whose subscribers was Robert Stephenson, have been put on record by Charles E. Lee, MA, FCIT, in a paper to the Newcomen Society for the Study of the History of Engineering and Technology and in his presidential address to the London Underground Railway Society. After construction of a system of tubes between

Euston station and the General Post Office the company was unable to persuade the powers-that-be to take interest in replacing street transport of the mails by Rammell's underground means. The Rammell passenger-carrying system, demonstrated as a sixpenny side show at Crystal Palace on a 600-yard line in a brickwork tunnel, was not connected with the Pneumatic Dispatch enterprise, but here again the inventor was luckless. The demonstration at Sydenham began on 27 August 1864. The idea was taken up for several short City railways, of which the Oxford Street & City was intended to make an underground line from Marble Arch under Oxford Street, New Oxford Street, High Holborn and Charterhouse Street to Farringdon Street on the Metropolitan and the Victoria Station & Thames Embankment undertaking proposed an underground line from Wilton Road, adjoining the cab yard in front of Victoria Station, passing under Victoria Street, Broad Sanctuary, St Margaret Street, New Palace Yard and Bridge Street to a terminus on the foreshore of the Thames at or near the northern side of the west end of Westminster Bridge; a second railway was to begin at the terminus of the first, and running under the Victoria Embankment, to end at or near Blackfriars Bridge on the western side of the northern end of the bridge. These two were rejected by the 1864 Committee. A third Rammell pneumatic line, for which the promoters just managed to deposit the Bill on the last day of November 1864, secured an Act on 5 July 1865 for a line ¾-mile long from Waterloo Station to a point near the Whitehall end of Great Scotland Yard. The air pressure on the Waterloo and Whitehall Railway was to have been about 22 lb per sq. ft, being alternately blow and suck, from the engine stationed at the Vine Street, Waterloo, end, with the carriages used as pistons in a 12 ft diameter tube. Alas, the financial débâcle of 1866 prevented the company raising the required funds although the total of these had been reduced by laying prefabricated tubes on the bed of the Thames in lieu of tunnelling. Eventually wound up in 1882, some of the company's assets are still buried under London and the Thames. Although the capacity of the line was put at 12,000 passengers an hour, the three vehicles specified (one loading, one unloading and one in transit) were four-wheelers with only 25 seats (20 third and 5 first class) and it is doubtful if the proposed terminal would have satisfied the lines of desire of Waterloo passengers seeking Trafalgar Square, the West End or connections via the District Railway, the station for which was placed on the Embankment at the river end of Villiers Street. It has to be remembered that when the Waterloo & Whitehall was planned neither the Victoria Embankment (opened 1870) nor Northumberland Avenue (opened 1876) were in existence. Although two London & South Western directors were on the board of the Waterloo & Whitehall Company the London & South Western Railway made no attempt to assist the smaller company which aimed at giving access from the South Western's somewhat remote terminus to the West End.

Among other proposals in Parliamentary Bill form which were turned down in 1864 the London Main Trunk Underground is of interest in that it sought to solve the Great Eastern's need for access to the City and West End by linking the Great Eastern main line round about its Coborn Road and Old Ford station by means of a line below Mile End Road, Aldgate and Fenchurch Street with the London, Chatham & Dover and by branches with the London & Blackwall and the Metropolitan Railways. The intentions were imposing: they were to construct railways to connect the railways on the north and south sides of the Thames; arrangements were sought with the London & North Western, Great Western, Great Northern, Great Eastern, Midland, North London, Blackwall, South Eastern, Brighton, South Western, Charing Cross, Metropolitan and Chatham & Dover Railways, Her Majesty's Commissioners of Woods, Forests & Land Revenues and Her Majesty's Commissioners of Works & Public Buildings, the Corporation of the City of London, the Commissioners of Sewers for the City of London, the Metropolitan Board of Works, gas and water companies, etc.

The Metropolitan Grand Union had ambitions very similar to the Metropolitan District Company for a line on an almost identical route round the south side of the Inner Circle, but it also proposed to make a link from Moorgate Metropolitan across the Thames west of the Tower of London on a bridge 100 ft above the water with a span of 820 ft and a descent to join the London & Greenwich viaduct near Spa Road station. The Thames viaduct was rejected and the first part of the project amalgamated with the Metropolitan District proposals for the Inner Circle, thus funnelling energy and finance towards the most essential objective.

The Charing Cross Northern and Charing Cross Western schemes both provided not only for railway construction but for finance to be raised and construction to be carried out by the major companies whose systems were to be linked up: the Great Northern, Midland, London & North Western, Great Eastern, South Eastern and Charing Cross for the Charing Cross Northern and the London & North Western, London, Brighton & South Coast, London & South Western, Great Western, South Eastern, Charing Cross and West London Extension companies in the case of the Charing Cross Western. The first was an underground scheme to join the Charing Cross near its terminus with the Great Northern, Midland and London & North Western Railways by means of a line along the route of the eastern part of Shaftesbury Avenue and running east of Southampton Row, splitting north of the Foundling Hospital to join the trunk lines north of Euston Road. The second was to have begun as a surface railway with a triangular junction with the Charing Cross near Waterloo and running parallel with the London & South Western Railway viaduct to a point south of Lambeth Bridge, where it would have crossed the Thames and gone underground about Vincent Square before travelling westward along the same trace as the Metropolitan District to the West London Extension, with a spur to Hammersmith.

Another line with Charing Cross in its title was to have been the Tottenham & Hampstead Junction (Extension to Charing Cross). The impecunious Tottenham & Hampstead Junction company had obtained an Act in 1862 for a line from the Hampstead Junction Railway (a satellite of the London & North Western) at Gospel Oak to the Northern & Eastern at Tottenham. The Great Eastern, as lessees of the Northern & Eastern, were interested, but it became evident that the London & North Western Railway was going to continue to route its traffic to the Great Eastern Railway and the Docks over the North London, of which it held two-thirds of the capital. With the energy of despair the Tottenham & Hampstead Junction, instead of giving up, entered upon a series of costly projects designed to extract traffic from other quarters. In 1863 it obtained powers to join the London extension of the Midland and now in 1864 it was anxious to make three new junctions with the Midland near Kentish Town and to project this line, which began east of Junction Road, to Camden Town where it entered tunnel to run by the modern Eversholt Street past Euston station, and by Southampton Row, to sweep round between the west side of Lincoln's Inn Fields and the east side of Covent Garden Market to terminate on the east side of the Charing Cross terminus of the Charing Cross Railway. This scheme relied on the powers to be given to the Midland, Great Northern, Great Eastern, London & North Western and South Eastern companies to raise the necessary cash and depended also upon working arrangements with those companies. Another project from the Tottenham & Hampstead Junction board room, not considered by the Select Committee whose work we are following, because it was outside the Metropolitan Railway District, was a scheme for a connection to Alexandra Palace and to the Great Northern main line about New Southgate (referred to as Colney Hatch) and in this the Edgware, Highgate & London company was joined as a source of possible finance.

The London Union, also among rejected proposals of 1864, proposed to join Hendon on the authorised Midland main line with Chelsea and in doing so to duplicate the West London and West London Extension Railways. It then proposed, by a tramway-sharp curve, to run in subway along the north bank, under Chelsea Embankment and Grosvenor Road, curving to emerge west of Millbank Prison and then to turn east and run as a surface railway to join the South Eastern Bricklayers' Arms branch. Other proposals would have joined Chelsea and Victoria Station; Victoria Station and Westminster; and Westminster with the Metropolitan Extension of the London, Chatham & Dover; a branch to Mansion House was also projected, and in all there were many resemblances to the generally successful Metropolitan District plans, which were approved except for the portion forming the outer circuit.

Last of the 1864 rejects to receive notice from the Committee was the Tottenham & Farringdon Street Railway, which was a comparatively straightforward project for a line to join the Northern & Eastern (and thus the Great Eastern system) with the London, Chatham & Dover and giving powers to those two companies and the Metropolitan. The projected trace was for a mainly surface railway from the neighbourhood of Coppermill Bridge over the River Lea, past Springfield Park, crossing Stamford Hill north of where Stoke Newington station now stands, rounding Abney Park and connecting by a north-to-west spur with the North London near Canonbury station. Thence it ran east of the Angel Islington crossroads and southwards to Farringdon Street on the Metropolitan.

Some of the proposals that had fallen through included the Cray Valley, a scheme for linking the North Kent line of the South Eastern at Erith with the Dartford Loop at Bexley and the London, Chatham & Dover at St Mary Cray, after which it hoped for connection to the South Eastern at Orpington and the London, Chatham & Dover (formerly the West End of London & Crystal Palace Farnborough Extension) never-to-be-built line at Farnborough. The London & Blackwall, Great Northern & Midland Junction had aimed at joining the London & Blackwall near Shadwell with Finsbury Park (Great Northern) and Kentish Town (Midland). The Mid-London was a project largely duplicating the Metropolitan and Metropolitan District proposals to link the West London at Kensington with the London, Chatham & Dover at Victoria and again north of Farringdon Street; there were also links to the Metropolitan at Paddington and the London & Blackwall at Fenchurch Street. The Walthamstow & City Terminus was merely a rival of the Walthamstow, Clapton & City; both began at Hale End and were to have used the North London's newly authorised Broad Street terminus and its branch from Dalston Junction.

The Bill for the Hampstead, Midland, North Western & Charing Cross Junction was interesting not only for providing yet another predecessor in theory of the Charing Cross, Euston & Hampstead tube of 1893, but for promising a subway for foot passengers under the Strand opposite Charing Cross terminus, an unfulfilled promise that has been made again in recent years, not by a railway but by the Greater London Council.

A first scheme for a steam-operated surface railway obtained its Act in 1864; the North Western & Charing Cross was to be subscribed for eagerly by the London & North Western and South Eastern Railways and was to construct a line from Hampstead Road to Charing Cross, with a branch to the London & North Western Railway and also to provide several new streets between Tottenham Court Road and the Strand. Of the twelve directors, four were nominated by the London & North Western Railway and four by the South Eastern Railway. The share capital was £900,000 with £330,000 on loan. An agreement between the London & North Western Railway and the South Eastern Railway was made on 21 May 1866 under which the North Western & Charing Cross was to raise the necessary capital and the shares were to be offered half to the South Eastern proprietors and half to the North Western proprietors.

An elaborate traffic agreement and machinery for fixing through rates and fares were prepared for the two companies and signed on 16 August 1866; by that time the financial crisis of that year was in full flight and it was deemed inadvisable to put money into this cross-London railway and the scheme was abandoned; although the Bill to effect this was prepared in 1868 the company failed to deposit it by 23 December of that year.

Three years passed before there was a revival as the London Central Railway Company. This postulated an underground line, with special provisions for a ventilation shaft in Leicester Square and the building of new streets between Oxford Street and the area on the north side of Trafalgar Square. The construction of Charing Cross Road from Trafalgar Square to St Giles's Circus was eventually completed in 1887 as one of the last tasks of the Metropolitan Board of Works before the formation of the London County Council. The London Central obtained its Act on 14 August 1871 and was intended to join both Euston and St Pancras to Charing Cross. The capital had risen to

£1,500,000 in shares and £500,000 on loan. The engineers were John Hawkshaw and John Wolfe-Barry. In July 1871 Agreements were made with the Board of Works, the Midland and the South Eastern Railways and signed by Basil Thomas Woodd, chairman of the London Central, and John Cator, also a promoter of the Bill, but money was not attracted to the proposal. Extension of time was sought in 1873 but in the end the promoters gave up the struggle to get the project off the ground. Eventually the Charing Cross, Euston & Hampstead deep-level tube railway occupied the route, linking the South Eastern and London & North Western termini, but without physical connection between the two main-line systems. The original Act for this railway was passed in 1893 and the scheme became feasible after the introduction of the Greathead shield for tunnelling through the solid blue London clay and the adoption of electric traction, pioneered by the City & South London Railway, which took up the scheme made successful by Dr Edward Hopkinson of Bessbrook and Newry experience. This combination acted as catalyst to a tube railway boom in the early 1890s that caused a joint Select Committee of both Houses of Parliament to be appointed to consider the schemes in 1892. The Charing Cross, Euston & Hampstead is also of interest as being the scheme which first caught the attention of Charles Tyson Yerkes and led to the actual construction of the three London Electric Railway tubes and the electrification of the Metropolitan District Railway.

That electrification sealed the fate of the deep-level District scheme, authorised on 6 August 1897, and intended to provide a link for high-speed tube trains from near Earl's Court over the 4¾ miles to Mansion House on a route below the District's shallow-tunnel alignment, with one intermediate station at Charing Cross. Subsequently an Act was obtained authorising the present South Kensington station of the Piccadilly Line, built as part of a flying junction to avoid work which would have been difficult later. One of the deep-level District platform tunnels was provided and hence the two landings for the Piccadilly line lifts at South Kensington which distinguished operations there until the escalators were installed. But the deep-level District with its distinctive means of speeding up operations by avoiding even calling at such a traffic centre as Victoria, had no place in the scheme of things after the District's capacity was so greatly enhanced by electrification, and no further construction was carried out, except in so far as the Piccadilly Line west of South Kensington is technically on its right-of-way. Another tube railway boom took effect in the beginning of the twentieth century.

Other notable attempts to provide internal railways in the Metropolitan Railway District which did not succeed included endeavours to link up with north-eastern suburbs, notably Tottenham and Walthamstow, and abortive attempts to develop railways in the South London suburbs and north-westward along the line of the Roman Watling Street—the modern Edgware Road.

In the 1860s there were proposals to serve the developing north-eastern suburbs by surface railways. The 1864 map prepared for the joint report of the Select Committee of the Houses of Parliament on Metropolitan Railways showed two lines emerging from the North London near Dalston Junction; one was the North London (Kingsland & Tottenham) which headed north through the Clapton Common area and the other the Walthamstow, Clapton & City, which took a course much more along the Lea Valley. It also proposed an extension northward from Walthamstow to Hale End. Yet another line relying on the North London for access to the City was the Walthamstow & City terminus but the Bill for this failed to be presented.

All these railways failed as schemes because the Great Eastern, in pursuing the City terminus project in which the Select Committee had encouraged it also included a new system of suburban lines. These provided in their final form for a short cut from the Northern & Eastern main line south of Tottenham through Clapton to Hackney Downs and Bethnal Green, a link from Enfield on the west of the Lea Valley to Hackney Downs and a branch from Seven Sisters to a station at Wood Green called Palace Gates. From Clapton a projection of the alignment from Hackney Downs served Walthamstow and Chingford. Proposals for a High Beech line, either from Loughton or as an extension of the Chingford branch were eventually dropped; no doubt the saving of Epping Forest as an open space, which an agitation of considerable weight achieved in 1882, robbed the area of its potential as a new and attractive dormitory zone.

The tube railway promotion era provided two more rival potential routes towards this part of outer London. These had several attempted incarnations; as will be seen there were several variations of route, starting in the 1890s with the London, Tottenham & Epping Forest of 1891, the London, Walthamstow & Epping Forest, which began in 1894, in 1895 promoted both variations of route and powers for abandonment. There was then a pause until the twentieth century was under way. The City & North East Suburban Electric proposed a line from Gracechurch Street, near its junction with Cornhill and Leadenhall Street, to Walthamstow, Epping Forest and Waltham Abbey serving the east side of the Lea Valley. There were proposals as to fares, working arrangements and other joint action with the Great Eastern and the City & South London. In 1901 it was suggested by Parliament that it should be diverted via Mile End Gate, Cambridge Heath and Leyton and in 1902 this route was criticised, especially in the early part where it ran under the line of the Whitechapel Road branch of the Metropolitan and Metropolitan District Joint City Lines & Extensions Railway so that the Bill was abandoned. The North East London Railway, also considered by Parliament in the 1901 session, proposed a line from Cannon Street to Page Green, Tottenham, near Tottenham High Cross, following the line of Kingsland Road via Bishopsgate and Stamford Hill; a branch from Stoke Newington to Walthamstow was proposed and, by means of an end-on junction with the Piccadilly & City Railway at Cannon Street, access was to be given to the West End. The line of this railway diverged from Cannon Street to run under Carter Lane before coming back to the alignment of Ludgate Hill, no doubt to give a wide berth to the foundations of St Paul's and to minimise the dangers foreseen by the ever-anxious Dean and Chapter. In a later version the line was diverted further away from the cathedral to Thames Street. These two were part of a trio of companies backed by the American Pierpont Morgan interests and eventually the end-on two were merged as the Piccadilly, City & North East London Railway and were joined with a project begun by the London United Tramways giving access to Hammersmith as the London Suburban Railway and from Tottenham this was projected north-westward to Southgate. These schemes lingered for discussion by the Royal Commission on London Traffic in 1905, when the Hammersmith, City & North East London Railway was shown with stations at Hammersmith Broadway, Brook Green, Addison Road, High Street, Albert Hall, Knightsbridge, Hyde Park Corner, St James's Street, Piccadilly Circus, Charing Cross, Wellington Street, Law Courts, Ludgate Circus, Cannon Street, Monument, Bishopsgate Street Without, Hackney Road, Kingsland Road (generating station along the Regent's Canal), Stamford Road, Shacklewell Lane, Gordon Road, Amhurst Park, High Road (Tottenham), Lordship Lane, Chequers Green and Palmers Green; from Gordon Road, a branch would have served Upper Clapton, Manor Road, Leyton Road, Grove Road, Shernhall Street (Walthamstow) and Chingford Road. This was opposed by the Yerkes group components of the Great Northern, Piccadilly & Brompton Railway and in the course of subsequent transactions the London United Tramways, shorn of its tube railway ambitions, became a part of the Underground

Electric Railways of London group and the Morgan interests withdrew from their extensive London programme.

The City & North East Suburban scheme of 1903 embraced branches from Mansion House and Monument, joining at Cornhill; then stations were proposed at Liverpool Street, Shoreditch, Hackney Road, Kingsland Road (generating station A on the Regent's Canal), Stamford Road, Arcola Street, Stoke Newington, Cazenove Road, Stamford Hill, The Avenue, Tottenham, and, in open air, Lordship Lane, White Hart Lane, and to a depot at Chequers Green. In this scheme the branch went from Hackney Road to Haggerston, Cambridge Road, and Victoria Park, Hackney (by Victoria Park North London station). Generating station sites B and C were placed either side of the Hackney Marshes and the line went on in the open from Temple Mills, to Leyton, Brewster Road, Lea Bridge Road, Walthamstow, Forest Road, Higham Hill, Chingford Hall, Chingford Green, Gilwell Park, Royal Oak, High Beech and Waltham Abbey. This east side of the Lea Valley is still unexploited. The placing of the proposed stations shows both a pathetic faith in the efficacy of regular half-mile spacing and a refusal to admit the traffic-generating characteristics of popular traffic centres.

One reaction from the tube railways promoted towards Tottenham and Walthamstow was that the Great Eastern Railway secured powers for electric traction and, wishing to save the raising of capital for that purpose, warned prospectors off the Great Eastern grass by a demonstration that a steam train could operate as fast as an electric and accelerate to 30 m.p.h. in 30 seconds. For this purpose the famous 0–10–0 three-cylinder tank engine No. 20 was built. Unfortunately the Decapod weighed 80 tons, concentrated on a 19 ft 6 in. wheelbase, and thus placed too heavy a burden on underline bridgework for the chief civil engineer's conscience and it did not enter regular service.

Great Eastern suburban conditions deteriorated fast after 1919 and extreme burdens were placed upon them by post-war developments in housing beyond Ilford and Wanstead, so much so that a very vigorous Ilford & District Railway Users' Association was formed, the activity of which culminated, after formation of the London Passenger Transport Board, in the Government-assisted 1935 plan for London tube railway extension and main-line suburban electrification. Ephemerally a Kearney tube was proposed from Aldgate, to Stratford, Ilford and the Becontree London County Council estate. On the Enfield and Chingford routes the intensive steam service, known as the 'Jazz' because of the three class distinctions on the coaches by coloured bands, mitigated the congestion by providing four trains every ten minutes in the peak.

South London, despite the claim by Colonel J. T. C. Moore-Brabazon (afterwards Lord Brabazon), when Minister of Transport, that railways 'looked like a madhouse on the map', had several routes that were intended paths for tube railways. One of these was the City & Brixton, which began as an independent project and was then taken over by the City & South London Railway. In its first form it was propounded as a scheme to pick up the former terminal line of the City & South London from King William Street to its junction under Borough High Street with the extension to Bank and Moorgate (opened 26 February 1900) and to project a line under Borough Road and Lambeth Road and thence via Kennington Road to an exchange station with the City & South London Railway at Oval and via Brixton Road to a point below the fourth milestone from Royal Exchange under Brixton Hill (just south of the Effra Road junction). An Act for this proposal was obtained on 1 July 1898. In 1899 powers were granted for a branch from Ingleton Street (near the junction of Angell Road and Brixton Road) to the depot of the City & South London Railway at Stockwell. In an endeavour to get the proposals off the ground possibilities of extension into the unrailed territory from Warlingham to Westerham were canvassed by a proposed City & Surrey Electric Railway Company, which also had a Caterham and Reigate branch in mind. To prevent such a takeover on its doorstep the City & South London company took action. By an Act of 11 August 1903 authority to take over the powers of the City & Brixton company was assumed by the City & South London company, with which there had been at least two directors in common with the City & Brixton company. By the time of the Royal Commission of 1905 it was possible to give the impression that a separate approach to Bank was intended, thus abrogating the purpose of using the City & South London Railway's original city terminal facilities. In the upshot none of the City & Brixton project was ever implemented.

From 1908 Elfric Wells Chalmers Kearney, inventor of a form of duo-rail with one rail above the train, vertically over the single running rail, and highly adapted to tube railway operation, proposed a line from Strand (in the crescent of Aldwych) to the Crystal Palace, with stations at Waterloo, Kennington Road, Oval, North Brixton, East Brixton, Herne Hill and Crystal Palace. No application for powers was made to Parliament.

Each station was to be on or near the surface and the track was to fall to a depth of about 110 ft on a gradient of 1 in 7 on leaving the stations, enabling gravity to supplement the electric power in accelerating the train to about 60 m.p.h.; the corresponding up grade to each station would assist the braking effort. With stations about a mile apart an all-stations train could maintain about 40 m.p.h.

From Oval, Kearney proposed a route via Victoria to Cricklewood. This had previously been before Parliament in various forms. In 1893 the Edgware Road & Victoria Railway Company was proposed, as an orthodox duo-rail tube. A start at Kilburn was intended and arrangements with the London & North Western, North London, Central London, Metropolitan District, London, Brighton & South Coast, London, Chatham & Dover and Victoria Station & Pimlico Railways were to be made. Why the Metropolitan Railway, which it also would have crossed, was left out of the list must be a mystery.

The North West London Railway had another try for an Edgware Road tube in 1899, proposing a line from Marble Arch to Cricklewood, but by 1906 we were back to square one with a Marble Arch & Cricklewood Railway proposing an extension to Victoria. From there the scheme first propounded in 1901 for a line from Victoria to Peckham as the Victoria, City & Southern, which would have had a Cannon Street branch, would have covered the route between Victoria and Oval which Kearney for some years advocated as one of his high-speed routes. The entire route from Peckham to Cricklewood has been covered for many years by a series of bus services, including, from the earliest days of the motor bus, the 2 minutes' headway on Service 16 from Victoria to Cricklewood which was maintained until recent difficulties in staffing London buses.

For Kearney's line to Cricklewood frequent stations were proposed starting at the Oval interchange with the Strand & Crystal Palace route. The sequence proposed was Vauxhall, Pimlico, Victoria (where the station would have been on the north side of the District platforms, wedged between the turn from Vauxhall Bridge Road and the curve towards Grosvenor Place), Hyde Park Corner (interchange with the Piccadilly), Marble Arch (interchange with the Central London), Edgware Road (interchange with the Metropolitan and the Bakerloo), Lords, Carlton Hill, Quex Road, Brondesbury (interchange with the Metropolitan at what was then known as Kilburn–Brondesbury) and Cricklewood. Victoria to Cricklewood was scheduled by Kearney at 10 minutes with seven stops, against an estimated 21 minutes for the $5\frac{1}{4}$ miles by conventional tube.

The Metropolitan secured powers in 1926 for a tube line from Kilburn to Edgware Road, but although indicators with spaces for stations north of Kilburn were installed at the rebuilt Edgware Road station, nothing else was done and the bottleneck between Finchley Road and Baker Street was eventually relieved by the arm of the Bakerloo, built by the London Passenger Transport Board. Previously the other branch of the Bakerloo, when extended from Paddington to Queen's Park with the aid of London & North Western Railway money, specifically avoided following Edgware Road, running parallel to it through Maida Vale Station below Randolph Avenue.

Another internal route which has attracted some attention is that between Paddington and Clapham Junction. A Bill, for example, was promoted in 1893 for a Clapham Junction & Paddington Railway as an underground line. Much more persistent were the promoters of the Latimer Road & Acton; powers were originally obtained in 1882 for a line of just over 2 miles in length from near Latimer Road on the Hammersmith & City to a station adjacent to the Great Western station at Acton. A certain amount of work was done more or less on the alignment of the modern Western Avenue and at one time casual inspection would reveal abutments of bridges over the North & South Western Junction at Acton, for example. But the capital of £180,000 in shares and £60,000 on loan was not raised and despite numerous extensions of time for acquiring the necessary lands and completing the works, the project faded away in the early years of the present century. The cause of the lack of interest by the money market is not far to seek; probably the route did not offer an alignment sufficiently different from the Great Western itself to offer prospects of serving a really remunerative new catchment area.

New areas to serve have, indeed, inspired several radial projects which in the end have failed to add to the railway resources around the Metropolis or which have developed in some different direction from the anticipations of the original promoters. Certain of these schemes have been remarkably resilient and have been presented to Parliament on several occasions, either to be rebuffed, or, if approved, to fail to merit the support of the share markets.

Perhaps the oldest of the radial routes were the pioneer projects of the London & Croydon and the South Eastern and its predecessors for a 'Mid-Kent' line which eventually produced a line entitled the Mid-Kent, but which for many years was an entry mainly to Surrey. A Central Kent scheme of 1836 was for a line via Sidcup, Sutton-at-Hone, Otford and Maidstone eastward. In 1845 the London & Croydon company, fearing a ganging up of the Brighton and South Eastern companies to avoid using its route from Croydon into London (Bricklayers' Arms branch had opened in 1844), making a frontal attack on the two bigger companies, proposed a line from Sydenham to Maidstone and Ashford, with a branch from Ightham to Tonbridge. The South Eastern proposed to shorten its roundabout main line, which followed the Brighton route to Redhill, by connecting the London & Greenwich with Paddock Wood via Ightham, with a branch from Ightham to Tonbridge. Neither plan, needless to say, came to fruition, but after the Mid-Kent was completed from Lewisham to Beckenham, apart from schemes for reaching Croydon – which produced the Mid-Kent line to Addiscombe and the London, Brighton & South Coast blocking line of the rather useless Central Croydon branch – there were three projects for reaching Brighton across the Kent–Surrey border country.

Directly south from New Beckenham the first of these proposals was the Beckenham, Lewes & Brighton, the prospectus of which was circulated in 1863. The preliminary negotiations for this began before the Mid-Kent secured its Act for extension to Addiscombe, so that between New Beckenham and Clock House it traverses a sharp reverse curve which would have enabled it to make a junction clearing it conveniently from the Beckenham, Lewes & Brighton main line. The Beckenham, Lewes & Brighton was to have gone via Park Langley, Biggin Hill, at the summit of the North Downs, Limpsfield, East Grinstead, Newick and Lewes to a terminus at Kemp Town. The London, Brighton & South Coast Railway promptly sought powers for a Kemp Town branch, granted in 1864, and built its blocking line at leisure, opening it on 2 August 1869. The distance by the Beckenham, Lewes & Brighton from Cannon Street to Brighton was estimated at 56 miles and the cost was put at £2,250,000. As well as services by the South Eastern from Cannon Street or London Bridge a link from the London, Chatham & Dover main line at Kent House was proposed and this was set out as the principal means of access in the *Bradshaw's Railway Manual* summary of the Parliamentary Bill. The House of Commons committee sat on the Beckenham, Lewes & Brighton Bill for twenty-five days before turning it down. In the following year branches to Westerham and Eastbourne were added to the scheme, but in 1864 the Bill was negatived without a division.

Two sessions later the London, Lewes & Brighton Railway Act received the Royal Assent on 6 August 1866. The scheme was generally similar to the Beckenham, Lewes & Brighton, beginning at Penge and Beckenham but differed in that the London, Chatham & Dover and South Eastern companies were given power to build the 55-mile line, which was to cost £2,250,000 in shares and £750,000 in loans. The financial crisis of 1866 would have made its survival very doubtful, but in any event the London, Chatham & Dover repudiated the plan straight away and the South Eastern stated that it could not be entertained until 1867. Without the anticipated financial support the project quickly faded out. Next revival came in 1876; the prospectus is before the writer and shows a scheme, now entitled the Metropolitan & Brighton Railway, for a line from Moorgate Street on the Metropolitan via the London, Chatham & Dover to Kent House or by the South Eastern (over the line from Blackfriars to Metropolitan Junction, authorised in 1872 and opened on 1 June 1878) through London Bridge and over the Mid-Kent to New Beckenham and thence via new line to Beckenham High Street, West Wickham, Warlingham, Caterham, Godstone, Blindley Heath, East Grinstead, West Hoathly, Lindfield, Haywards Heath, St John's, Hurstpierpoint, Newtimber and Patcham to a terminus at Brighton Pavilion, approached over a viaduct. This scheme was another that did not make the grade, despite the rise in the population of Brighton from 31,000 in 1831 to 87,000 in 1861.

The area between Beckenham and Westerham has remained without a north-south railway to this day, although a scheme backed by the Southern Railway, the Southern Heights, was proposed in 1925, when a Light Railway Order was sought on 27 November. The following year the Southern board decided to guarantee interest on £300,000 of debentures at 5 per cent and to provide £140,000 of capital to electrify the line. It would have extended from Orpington 15¾ miles via Tatsfield to Sanderstead and would have been single track. There would have been stations at Green Street Green, Downe and Keston, Cudham and Biggin Hill, Westerham Hill, Tatsfield, Chelsham, Hamsey Green, and Mitchley Wood. By 1931 the powers had lapsed without any construction having taken place and because of the imminence of the formation of the London Passenger Transport Board and of pooling of receipts between the Board and the main-line railways, the Southern Railway was no longer anxious to take on a line for development in the London Passenger Transport Board area for which it could see no certain prospects.

Other radial railways on the south which proved abortive included the Guildford, Kingston & London of 1881, a promotion in the London terminus of which the Metropolitan District Railway took a close interest. From Guildford to near Surbiton the Guildford, Kingston & London had the route approximately of the Southern's new Guildford line. Then it was to have skirted Kingston and, going via Kingston Vale and between Wimbledon Common and Putney Heath, to have joined the District at Putney Bridge, where it had arrived from West Brompton in 1880. The District offered the Guildford, Kingston & London an elaborate terminal site at Pelham Place, South Kensington, but not unnaturally the London & South Western resented an invasion of its territory and the upshot after negotiation was provision by the London & South Western Railway of a line from terminal platforms at Wimbledon to Putney Bridge for use by District trains, a spur from East Putney to Wandsworth, used by a London & South Western Railway service from Waterloo to Wimbledon and the new Guildford line, from just beyond Surbiton, served with the Leatherhead–Effingham link, by London & South Western Railway trains. District trains were projected to Wimbledon from 3 June 1889 and the London & South Western Railway's own service via East Putney on 1 July 1889. To make sure of its blocking line from Hampton Court Junction and Leatherhead via Effingham to Guildford the London & South Western Railway had pressed on regardless and opened their new section on 2 February 1885.

West of Guildford an attempt was made in 1895 to raise interest in the Portsmouth, Basingstoke & Godalming Railway which was intended to split the space between the Portsmouth line and the main line to Southampton. The Guildford arm of this railway was intended to start by a triangular junction with the South Eastern line between Guildford and Shalford and to run via Godalming, Elstead, Tilford, Frensham and Selborne to a junction with the Basingstoke–Portsmouth section about East Tisted. The prospectus shows clearly the flimsy basis on which many railway company promotions were made. From a solemn statistical table the deduction is made that four South of England railways (London & South Western Railway, London, Brighton & South Coast Railway, South Eastern Railway and London, Chatham & Dover Railway) had average gross earnings in the half year to June 1895 averaging £4,673 a mile; for the 69 miles of the new railway that average would give a total of £322,437 average yearly gross receipts. From that 33 per cent is deducted because the new railway would not have the following advantages: (a) a London terminus; (b) a London district traffic; (c) a Continental steamboat traffic; (d) an equal number of populated towns. This would leave an estimated revenue of £216,033; deduction of 55 per cent working expenses would leave £97,215 of which £96,000 would be absorbed by 4 per cent per annum on £600,000 debentures (£24,000), leaving a 4 per cent dividend on the Ordinary Capital of £1,800,000 (£72,000). It was not only amazing that any promoter would think such an argument likely to persuade the Stock Exchange of the merits of such a railway, but still more extraordinary that the London & South Western board took it sufficiently seriously to promote two blocking lines (the Meon Valley Railway and the Basingstoke & Alton Light Railway), although nothing was done to fill up the delectable country between Guildford and Selborne.

The following year there was another attack on a vacant piece of London & South Western Railway territory with the prospectus of the Basingstoke & Wokingham Railway through Sherfield-upon-Loddon, Eversley and Barkham. This would have given the London & South Western Railway yet another link from the Staines and Ascot route to the main line at Basingstoke additional to the West Byfleet junctions or via Frimley and the Sturt Lane triangle, but practical value did not seem a paramount consideration.

The sector of the Chiltern Hills between the original Great Western main line and the London & North Western main line was filled after many attempts by the Extension Line of the Metropolitan Railway, which reached Aylesbury and thus Verney Junction on 1 September 1892. But there remained a considerable area along the Oxford Road between Uxbridge and High Wycombe unserved by rail. A plan was approved in 1850 by the shareholders of the Oxford, Worcester & Wolverhampton Railway for an independent line to the Metropolis. A station at St Giles, Oxford, was to have been followed by Bledlow (with an Aylesbury branch), Princes Risborough, High Wycombe, Beaconsfield, Gerrard's Cross, Denham, Uxbridge, West Drayton, Cranford, Heston and Brentford. The intended junction at Brentford was with the London & South Western Railway, near the $10\frac{1}{2}$ mile post from London. In 1853 a shorter route from Uxbridge, via Hayes and Southall to Brentford was proposed, and at the same time a connection to the London & North Western Railway at Willesden via Perivale was advocated and the outlet to the London & South Western Railway seemed less pressing, although another possible course seemed to be to join with the West End of London & Crystal Palace and the rather shadowy Millbank terminus proposal that eventually crystallised as the Victoria Station & Pimlico undertaking at the end of the decade.

Parliament failed to pass this scheme in 1851 and in 1852 considered it again as the London & Mid-Western; in 1853 it also included an Oxford and Cheltenham line, but the Act again failed to pass after a committee reviewed it and a rival North Western project. In the end a connection at Yarnton from the London & North Western Railway Bletchley–Oxford line to the Oxford, Worcester & Wolverhampton gave that company the outlet it sought to Euston, and even into London, Midland & Scottish days the curve at Bletchley from the main line towards Oxford was called the Worcester Curve, although by then it was overlaid with the sidings of a brickworks.

In the 1890s many South Wales businessmen were anxious to break the monopoly of London traffic enjoyed by the Great Western, and promoters connected with the Barry Railway were singularly lively. A combination of circumstances made the promotion of a Bill for a London & South Wales Railway possible; in 1893 a link with the London & South Western Railway was favoured, but in 1895 a Bill was deposited for 163 miles of line at an estimated cost of £5,688,252, beginning with a junction with the Barry Railway and running via Cardiff, Caerwent and Beachley to Malmesbury, Cricklade and, skirting Oxford, to go to Bledlow. Here the trunk route went on to Great Missenden on the Metropolitan and another arm was projected to Welsh Harp, Hendon on the Midland, via High Wycombe, Beaconsfield, Denham, Ruislip and across the London & North Western Railway just south of Harrow & Wealdstone. Running powers to the London terminus of what was still the Manchester, Sheffield & Lincolnshire Railway were proposed and also into St Pancras over the Midland.

The District, ever eager to slight the Metropolitan, now took a hand by putting in two Bills in 1896. One was for an extension of the Ealing & South Harrow, sanctioned in 1894, to Uxbridge, Gerrard's Cross, Beaconsfield and High Wycombe, running beyond Gerrard's Cross parallel to the route of the London & South Wales Welsh Harp branch. Despite the dog-leg course of this extension of the Ealing & South Harrow in the Uxbridge area, it was hoped to attract the London & South Wales to the Pelham Place site intended for the Guildford, Kingston & London back in 1881, but on a more grandiose scale. A separate terminal spur would have left west of South Kensington District platforms and a large area of property was scheduled for demolition.

The District company cooled off from the South Kensington terminal idea within weeks and the Ealing & South Harrow extension proposal was cut back to Uxbridge. In 1897 a modified route, more like that afterwards taken by the Metropolitan Uxbridge branch, was sought with an extension to High Wycombe, but by this time the Great Western was fully alerted to the claims of its competitors. South Wales interests were met by the Great Western direct Badminton line from Wootton Bassett to the Severn Tunnel approach, for which an Act was obtained on 7 August 1896, within a few weeks of the London & South Wales promoters having capitulated. The cut-off on the Birmingham line, crossing the Chilterns via Beaconsfield, High Wycombe and Princes Risborough, and starting off close in to London at Old Oak Common, was sanctioned on 6 August 1897 in respect of the Acton & Wycombe portion and effectively prevented District extensions towards the lush and developable country in the Chiltern Hills.

Another of the might-have-been routes on radial lines from the London area lies north-east of Ongar, where a projection into deepest Essex, via Dunmow, was canvassed as the route of a light railway through the Rodings with a possible extension to Great Bardfield, intended as the terminus of the Great Eastern's Elsenham & Thaxted Light Railway. When the First World War was over the Light Railways Syndicate made an application for a line in a fresh direction from Ongar, over the $8\frac{1}{4}$ miles from Chipping Ongar to Shenfield on the Great Eastern main line, it being proposed to incorporate an Ongar & Shenfield Light Railway Company for the purpose. The line would have been single and a spur would have run alongside the Great Eastern main line at Shenfield without effecting a junction, but it was proposed to join the Southend branch somewhere east of the station.

Another class of railway project was the peripheral venture that would have carried out some or all of the objects of the Metropolitan District's ill-fated Outer Circle scheme. Many promoters were quite certain that there was a fortune for a railway which would join up the main lines outside the built-up area.

Charles Grey Mott, a director of the Great Western and chairman of the City & South London, was instrumental in the formation of the Metropolitan Outer Circle, which obtained its Act on 7 August 1888. It was authorised to begin with a junction with the Ealing branch of the Metropolitan District and with the Great Western at Ealing and to go to a triangular junction with the Great Eastern Cambridge line at Tottenham, joining on the way the North & South Western Junction, the Metropolitan, the Midland at Hendon, and the Great Northern at Southgate. Capital was authorised at £1,200,000 in £10 shares and £400,000 could be raised by borrowing. The period for the completion of works was five years, but in 1891 permission had to be sought for extension of time for completion and another application was made in 1893 for an extension of time until 7 August 1896. Before that, however, the railway had made an application to abandon the works granted by the 1888 Act and the Royal Assent to the process of winding up the company's affairs was granted on 14 May 1895.

1 Approaches to the south-east London railway terminals in the 1930s, showing London Bridge and, top right, Cannon Street.

2   London Bridge, London, Brighton & South Coast Railway, April 1882.

3 The SER connection at Waterloo, constructed between platforms 1 and 2 in 1864: it carried the short-lived Cannon Street–Kensington (Addison Road) service in the mid-1860s, and later the Willesden Junction–Waterloo service operated briefly by the LNWR. Otherwise the line was used only for occasional stock movements, and by trains carrying Queen Victoria from Windsor to the Channel ports.

4 *above left* Sir John Hawkshaw's train shed at Charing Cross soon after
the station was opened. A flaw in the welding of the roof led to its collapse
forty-two years later, on 5 December 1905.

5 *below left* The Great Hall at Cannon Street: built by Hawkshaw for the
SER and opened in 1866; damaged by bombing, 10/11 May 1941;
demolished 1963.

6 *above right* End of the broad gauge at Clapham Junction, between
platforms 16 and 17, in the 1860s.

7 *above left*   NLR 4–4–0 tank no. 13, built by Adams at Bow, 1869, seen at Broad Street heading a train to the Great Northern's Alexandra Palace branch (now a nature reserve).

8 *above right*   One of the Port of London Authority's diminutive Manning Wardle 2–4–0 tanks at North Greenwich, while running round a Millwall Extension Line train.

9 *below right*   Outer Circle train of LNWR teak four-wheelers at Kensington (Addison Road) hauled by a 2–4–2 condensing tank engine.

10   GWR pannier tank (fitted with condensing apparatus for working to Smithfield) approaching Kensington Olympia with a van train.

11 One of Park's NLR 0–6–0 tanks on a transfer freight near Millwall
Junction.

12 Ex-LMSR 'Jinty' and GNR saddle tank at Blackwall Junction, 1957.

13 LMSR Broad Street–Poplar train at Hackney, 1927.

14   Last vestige of the Euston–Croydon service: a LMSR parcels train arrives at East Croydon, 1937.

15   Freight from the docks, hauled by ex-GNR saddle tank, near Dalston Junction, 1958.

16 *left* Dalston Junction box in 1965—one time key point of North London passenger services.

17 *above right* Platforms 3 and 4 at Dalston Junction, 1950.

18 *centre right* London Midland Region freight at Gospel Oak, on the former Hampstead Junction Railway, headed by an 850 h.p. diesel locomotive.

19 *below right* Willesden Junction High Level platforms in the 1950s.

20 *left* The Great Hall, Euston: designed by P. C. Hardwick for the London & North Western Railway. Opened 1849; demolished 1963.

21 *above* Euston Station before its reconstruction: platforms 5, 6 and 7, showing third and fourth rail electrification for the Watford service.

22 *left*   Former GNR condensing 0–6–2 tank on a freight train from the
Widened Lines to the south of the Thames, passing the remains of Snow
Hill Station, 1952.

23 *above*   GNR J50 class 0–6–0T heads a train from the Widened Lines
to the Southern up the bank past Holborn Viaduct platforms, 1954.

24 The scene from Blackfriars box in July 1970, with the bridge over the
Thames reduced to two tracks. A Sevenoaks via Catford Loop train is
leaving.

25 A Midland 0–6–0T at Walworth Coal Sidings on the LC&DR city line, 1957.

26 *above left* Steam train from the Mid-Kent line in bay at Beckenham Junction, Southern Railway, 1926.

27 *above right* Blackfriars–Crystal Palace train emerging from Crescent Wood tunnel to call at Upper Sydenham.

28 *below right* The massive proportions of Crystal Palace High Level terminus.

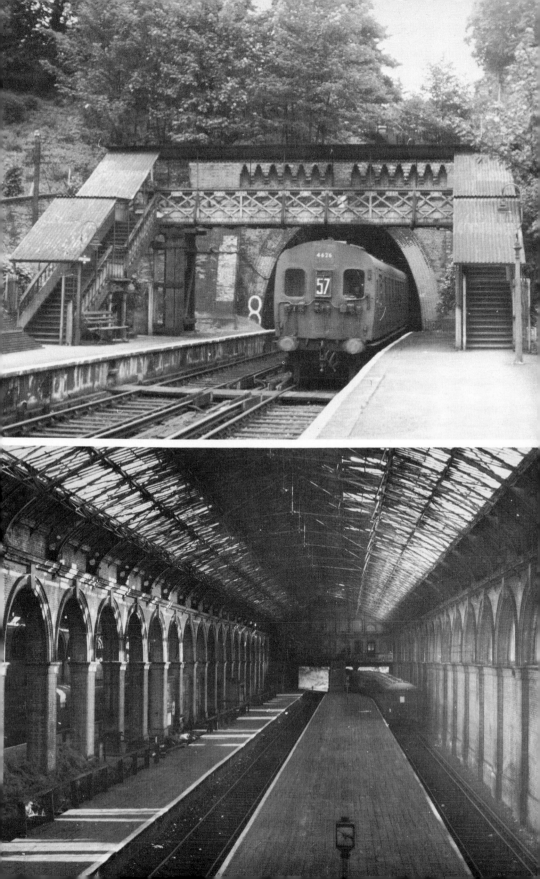

29 *above left* Southern Railway Wimbledon–Ludgate Hill via Merton Abbey train, at Merton Park just before the abandonment of the south side of Wimbledon–Tooting loop for passenger services in March 1929.

30 *below left* Eastern Region Moorgate–New Barnet train at Farringdon (London Transport) station, with wagons in the background at the LNER's former City goods depot.

31 *above right* GNR 0–4–4T no. 523 climbing the Northern Heights at Crouch End, 1900. In 1974 the cutting was the proposed site of a housing scheme, but this was rejected by popular acclaim early in 1975.

32 Moorgate Metropolitan in March 1960, showing bays for Metropolitan
Line terminating trains. Platforms for Midland and GNR trains on the
Widened Lines, to the left.

33   In May 1964 the Metropolitan Line was diverted between Barbican
and Moorgate to make room for the City Corporation's Barbican
development. The new Moorgate station is under the arrow; in line with
it is the site of the Whitecross Street depot, closed in 1936 and destroyed
during a German raid in 1940.

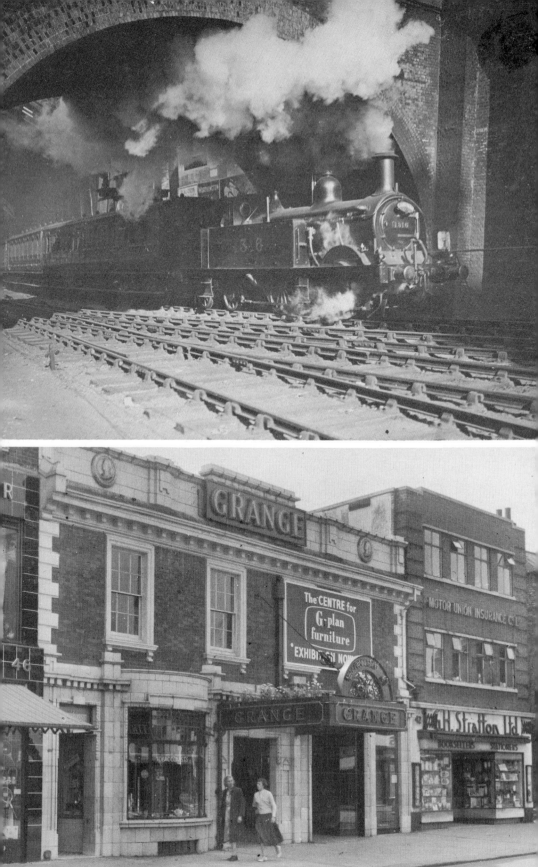

34 *above left* Midland Railway 0–4–4T leaving Farringdon Street for
Barbican and Moorgate Street on the Metropolitan Widened Lines.

35 *below left* A railway that never was: the Grange furniture store in
Watford High Street was built for adaptation as a Metropolitan station, but
no railway was ever built to it.

36 *above right* Replacing the bridge over the Surrey Canal on the East
London line, 1950.

37 *above left* Royal Albert Dock Railway train for Custom House
(Great Eastern) at Gallions, before 1896. The engine is an Allan type,
built at Crewe in 1849, and sold out of LNWR service in 1882.

38 *above right* West Brompton, Metropolitan District Railway, with
4–4–0T no. 10, 1876.

39 *below right* Metropolitan Extension Line train of rigid eight-wheeled
stock hauled by 0–4–4T no. 77, after electrification of the line to Harrow
and Uxbridge.

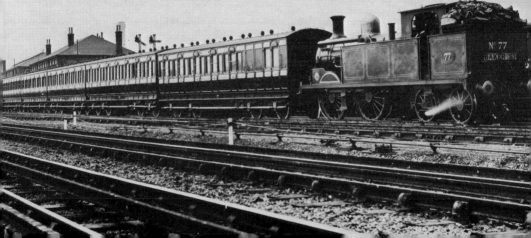

40 *above left* Building a tube railway and its overground connections: working site at Newbury Park; eastbound track looking west, showing 12 ft 3 in. diameter cast-iron lining constructed in trench. The work, interrupted by the Second World War, is seen in July 1948, with the GER tracks to Seven Kings and Ilford still *in situ*.

41 *above right* The Great Eastern Railway's experimental 0–10–0 tank engine, designed to outvie electric traction.

42 *below right* A Great Eastern 0–6–2 tank on a North Woolwich–Stratford train accelerates from Canning Town, 1962.

43   The London Necropolis Company's station at 121, Westminster Bridge
Road, opened in 1902 to serve their cemetery at Brookwood, near Woking,
via the LSWR; destroyed by bombing, May 1941.

There were, however, a number of railways of similar objects. The Greater London Railway was promoted during 1910; it was to begin on the London & South Western at Feltham and make connections with all the main lines north of the Thames, at a cost of £2,300,000. The projected mileage was 57 and it was to have extended to Tilbury, with a connection to the Port of London Authority railways at Victoria Dock. An unusual feature of the proposed connections was a junction with the then projected extension of the Hampstead tube, north of Golders Green, on its way to Edgware. Principal railway company witness against its Bill was Herbert Ashcombe Walker, soon to become general manager of the London & South Western Railway. In 1913 the scheme came up again as the much shorter Northern Junction Railway, designed to link Brentford on the London & South Western Railway with Wood Green on the Great Northern, 17¾ miles distant. There was to have been a link with the Great Central Railway and junctions also with the Metropolitan and Metropolitan District Railways. The Midland and London & North Western Railways joined forces in producing evidence against the Northern Junction Railway, because they were satisfied with their existing connections. The Northern Junction Railway made another fundamental error. Its route was laid out across the nascent Hampstead Garden Suburb and much vituperation from influential people was produced against the would-be desecrators of the environment. Therefore, in 1914 when the Bill was rejected, there was much rejoicing in the highways and byways of the garden suburb, which until 1974 was not even penetrated by a bus service from Golders Green tube station. An additional example of this sort of northern junction line on a more limited scale is afforded by the North Western & Ealing, the promoters of which sought an Act in the Parliamentary session of 1887.

After the railway grouping in 1923 rationalisation of freight operation around London was achieved to some extent, but the most notable feature of the post-war period was a spread of suburban housing and a great expansion of suburban passenger services. The four general managers decided to look afresh at the Outer Circle Railway scheme, choosing a new route free from the trammels of suburban housing. At 1930 prices a 63-mile line would have cost £9,700,000, of which £2,500,000 would have been for land purchase and compensation. Further out over some of its route than any previous scheme, it ran from Feltham on the Southern to the Port of London Authority at Victoria Dock, with a Wanstead–Tilbury branch; there were to be junctions with the Great Western, the London & North Western section of the London, Midland and Scottish, the Metropolitan & Great Central Joint, the Midland section of the London, Midland & Scottish, the Great Northern and Great Eastern sections of the London & North Eastern Railway and the Tilbury section of the London, Midland & Scottish. The cost of electrification was not included in the cost of the line, although electric traction was thought vital, and another dichotomy was that it was thought traffic (passenger and local freight) would be less than the cost of such a railway would justify; the exchange traffic would be diverted from existing routes which were already satisfactory. Use of the new route would involve the companies in loss of revenue. To earn 6 per cent on the capital would have necessitated a revenue of £47,000 or more a mile on the new railway or five times what the two most prosperous groups took per mile of route. There was thus no justification for such a scheme. Its absence was probably regretted during the Second World War, but for how long after the formation of British Railways such regret lasted is very doubtful.

A further scheme for links between the main lines north of the Thames had the Regent's Canal for a basis. During 1846 and the subsequent session of Parliament the canal company wished to get on the railway band wagon with a line of its own from Paddington to the Docks, but the Government intimated its horror at the idea of a railway through Regent's Park and the canal company's Bill was withdrawn. The idea was talked about for three decades and in 1882 on 18 August the Royal Assent was given to a Bill for the transfer of the canal to the Regent's Canal City & Docks Railway Company and the construction of railways from the Great Western at Paddington to the City and on to the Royal Albert Dock of the London & St Katherine Docks Company. Connections were to be made with the Midland Railway and the Great Northern Railway at St Pancras and King's Cross respectively. In August 1883 two Acts were passed, one constituting the canal undertaking a separate body with a separate capital of £1,500,000 in shares or stock and £190,000 on mortgage, and the second making another separate undertaking of the railways between the Midland and Great Northern systems and the City (Barbican) to be known as the City Lines Undertaking. As James Staats Forbes, chairman of the Metropolitan District Railway, was chairman of the Regent's Canal Railway, it can be seen as a plot for taking business from the Widened Lines of the Metropolitan, of which the chairman was Sir Edward Watkin, an old enemy of Forbes. Nothing was ever done towards construction of these railways, but there were numerous financial manoeuvres towards the raising of the cash and even in 1892 a further attack on the

Metropolitan position by renaming the company the North Metropolitan Railway & Canal Company at the same time that part of the railway scheme was thrown overboard and abandoned.

By contrast with the northern sector of the London junction schemes there were few on the south of the Thames. One abortive plan, similar to the turning of the Regent's Canal into a railway, was for a West London Extension & Surrey Commercial Docks Railway which proposed junctions with the Brighton, South Eastern and East London Railways in 1887, abandonment of the Grand Surrey Canal, which provided a direct course from Camberwell to the neighbourhood of the Surrey docks, and proposed agreements with practically every railway entering the Metropolis.

A railway route that looks a 'natural' for a sort of English 'Grande Ceinture' around the north of the capital extends up the Lea Valley, across from Hertford to Hatfield and St Albans and then down the Colne Valley to the Thames. There were communications between the Great Eastern and Great Northern at Hertford, a somewhat unsatisfactory juxtaposition of the Hertford and St Albans branches of the Great Northern at Hatfield, a common terminal of the Great Northern and London & North Western at St Albans, a backshunt connection at Watford Junction from the London & North Western Railway St Albans and Rickmansworth branches and thence a gap from Rickmansworth to Uxbridge, partially filled by the line from the Great Western and Great Central Joint Railway near Denham to Uxbridge High Street. When this railway was opened on 1 May 1907 it ended, south of High Street station, in a girder bridge over the Oxford Road which led nowhere; the intended Great Western connection to the West Drayton and Uxbridge Vine Street branch was never carried out. During the First World War someone recovered the useless girder bridge for real service elsewhere. The Great Western had also built a branch from West Drayton to Staines which ephemerally, under the stress of war, served for through communication to the London & South Western.

The gap in the Colne Valley has seen many essays at its closure. The Uxbridge & Rickmansworth was first incorporated on 28 June 1861 for 8 miles 13 chains of line from the Great Western at Uxbridge to join the Watford & Rickmansworth at Rickmansworth, with a branch to Scot's Bridge Mills. The capital was then put at £70,000 in £10 shares and loans up to £23,000 were sanctioned. In 1862 a deviation was authorised, but the works were to be completed by 28 June 1864. In 1863 an extension of time was sought and obtained to 1 January 1866.

Yet another extension, on 28 June 1866, permitted the works to be completed by 28 June 1868. Additional capital was £43,000 in shares and £14,000 on loan. A fourth extension was granted in 1868 and in 1873, whereas earlier the works had been reported 'in progress', the company was stated to be in liquidation.

A new company with a different board of directors and a fresh set of officers was incorporated on 11 August 1881, and may be taken as typical of the increase in costs towards the end of Victoria's reign. The 8 miles of railway authorised on this occasion were to involve a capital of £144,000 in £10 shares and borrowing powers were included for a further £48,000. Five years were allowed for completion, so to keep the scheme alive an Act was obtained in 1884 to extend the time for purchase of land to 11 August 1885. Another Act of 1886 gave authority for deviation among other purposes with £25,000 new capital and £3,333 additional loans. But the project never got off the ground, and even the mighty Great Western eventually lost interest in its scheme for a Paddington–Uxbridge–Paddington roundabout outer suburban service, despite another promotion in 1895 of a fresh Uxbridge & Rickmansworth Railway.

five

DEVELOPING THE NORTH LONDON AGAIN

The sad state of the North London passenger business is the concern of many outside that railway's sphere of influence and many again who knew not the days of North London prosperity. Some of its Victorian success was almost accidental; it was designed to give the London & Birmingham access to the West India Docks, and by the time it was completed it was not only the dock outlet at the London end of the mighty London & North Western Railway but a trade was waiting to be picked up in distribution of seaborne coal from the Docks to London suburbs and this it did by handing over its coal distribution business to the Northumberland and Durham Coal Company which provided its own engines and wagons for handling coal from Thames-side quays to the North London depots. Too late the North London board realised the obstruction to its own business this would cause and in 1854 it had to buy out its eager contractor for £10,000 in hard cash. But it had not only the freight business due to its position as an outlet for the London & North Western to the Docks, to Haydon Square on the London & Blackwall and to the London & North Western Railway depot at Broad Street, but the traffic bound for the Great Eastern and from the Great Western, the Great Northern and the Midland for similar destinations.

Quite surprisingly the North London turned out to be a remunerative passenger line, its own stations producing traffic first for Fenchurch Street and then for Broad Street. The Poplar branch generated an extensive traffic of its own and the North London trains were soon gathering passengers from the London & North Western suburban area, the Hampstead Junction line and the North & South Western Junction Railway and its London & South Western connections. After 1875 a considerable part of Great Northern suburban business was handled at Broad Street.

This happy state of affairs and the dividends that accompanied them definitely ended with the nineteenth century. Before that the horse tram and the horse bus had made some inroads into North London traffic owing to the circuitous nature of many of its routes and the sharp peaks of the flows from and to Great Northern suburban stations. Then came short cuts by underground with the joining of the District and Tilbury systems by the Whitechapel & Bow Railway, London's last shallow underground. It formed a chord across the wide loop of the Broad Street, Bow and Poplar route of the North London between the City and Bow and Bromley and although it opened for steam traction in 1902, the journey time was less than on the North London. By 1905 electric trains were operating and the time from Mansion House to Bow Road came down to less than 15 minutes, against the best part of half an hour on a hard-wooden-seated North London third from Broad Street to Bow. Another blow fell in 1904 with the opening of the Great Northern & City tube from Finsbury Park to Moorgate. By this the maximum journey time was 13 minutes and at some parts of the peak hours the run was only 11 minutes, against 18 minutes from Finsbury Park to Broad Street. Then the swing towards business in the West End was accelerated by the Piccadilly tube which took passengers from Finsbury Park to places for which the North London had no service; the Hampstead tube was another quick, rapid-transit short cut in 1907. By 1908 the North London was punch-drunk and its principal proprietor (the London & North Western Railway held two-thirds of the capital) thought its affairs should be run more economically as a department of the London & North Western Railway.

Economies were effected, but at the cost of sapping the morale of the North London men, with their proud construction and maintenance record at Bow reduced to the status of a North Western motive power depot and the North London traffic manager a mere London & North Western district officer, as the decimated North London staff, perhaps wrong-headedly, felt. This left the railway in no state to meet the sharper competition of the motor bus which developed after viability was achieved by that medium following introduction later in 1910 of the B-type bus by the London General Omnibus Company. The full force of electric tramway competition was felt after 1910 with introduction of through-running between the London County Council and suburban tramways and the completion of the London County Council network conversion from horse to electric traction. No attempt was made to shorten North London journey times or to provide more comfortable rolling stock. The London & North Western Railway electrification, thought of in 1911, was with leisurely running stock and did not include the Poplar line. It took until 1916 to materialise on the Richmond service; in 1914 the track was ready from Willesden Junction to Earl's Court, but District trains had to be borrowed for operation. In 1913 a ninth platform had been optimistically added to accommodation for trains at the Broad Street terminus. Some of the wounds the North London sustained in the battle to retain its traffic were self-inflicted. The railway was closed down for days at a time while urgent consignments were handled for shipment at West India Docks during the war. The same ideology would have closed down the Southern passenger service entirely for a period preceding D-day in 1944, but in fact, by realistic operating methods, the Southern did not cancel any passenger trains at that critical period and shifted the vital freight and other military traffic without any delays simply by the resolve of its traffic department to surmount difficulties.

Between the wars the London, Midland & Scottish took over the North London in 1923 and control became even more remote than in London & North Western Railway days. The staff became quite dispirited, so that about 1930 when the writer took an Australian friend to Bow station with a view to riding to Poplar, the booking clerk snapped: 'Why don't you get a bloody bus?' and banged down his guichet window. It was at this period that the greedy London, Midland & Scottish estates department neglected the cleaning, painting and signing of the stations and made it quite difficult to find some of them. A row of shops built in Highbury station yard obscured the view of the distinctive station building. Signs giving the direction to stations, put up by the Southern in its suburban areas, for example, seemed to be taboo in London, Midland & Scottish areas and there were complaints about the difficulty of finding Finchley Road and Frognal station, the entrance to which was cleverly hidden.

During the Second World War the North London had a full share of the physical battering sustained by London railways and in the wisdom of the London, Midland & Scottish its passenger train service between Dalston and Poplar was brought to an end on 15 May 1944, but passengers were conveyed by special bus to the stations on the route until war activity was virtually over in the following spring.

The Broad Street to Richmond service has been threatened on more than one occasion. British Railways at one time had designs upon it because of a parcels train project; the economics of the service caused reductions first of all of service and then of train lengths. The Kew Bridge branch service ended in 1940 and the conductor rail was soon afterwards lifted.

[74]

At various times, also during 1940, some of the intermediate stations were closed, including Shoreditch and Haggerston. Vandals burned down Kentish Town West station during 1971. A reduction of passenger interest under British Railways auspices can also be attributed to the strict enforcement of passenger fares on a mileage basis, even when the North London route was longer than competing services. Even freight has been reduced with the closing of the London & North Western Railway goods depot at Broad Street in 1969 and the lessening of Port of London Authority interest in the inner London docks. Furthermore the 100-year-old bridge at Kew on the Gunnersbury–Richmond section is no longer deemed suitable for the pounding of locomotives, whether steam or diesel-electric, so that freight diverges from the North & South Western junction at Acton to Kew and Hounslow when bound for the Southern Region.

For many reasons a large cross-section of the general public would like to see the Broad Street–Richmond service restored to prosperity and included in British Rail development programmes. This is the reason for the existence of the North London Line Committee, chaired by Mrs K. Peacock of Hampstead and of which the honorary secretary in 1974 was Miss M. Reed. They looked with satisfaction to the political changes on the Greater London Council which produced greater interest in public transport, and look forward as a result of that, and of Government policy, to the allocation of money to what has been called, on provincial British Rail lines serving commuters in passenger transport authority areas, 'up-grading' of the North London Line. Posters designed to promote North London travel have been issued and are purchased by devotees at fifteen pence each for exhibition in windows of private houses. The proposals put in evidence to the Rail Study Group included re-opening of certain closed stations and the introduction of certain new ones. Brian Braddon, honorary treasurer of the North London Line Committee, in a pamphlet upon the potential development of the North London Line, suggests that the utility of the North London Line is not merely as a readymade route for part of an Outer Circle railway, although it figures in several schemes. It is capable of development in its own right. What is advocated is operation and publicity as if it were a London Transport Executive railway (more frequent services and inclusion on the London Underground map, as many potential users do not appear to know of its existence; better direction notices to stations and a more prominent style of external announcement of their location) and a series of additions to the stopping places so that more and better traffic centres are served.

Broad Street is, of course, in a splendid position in the City of London, near Finsbury Circus and about half a mile north of the Bank of England–Mansion House junction. It is served by the Metropolitan and Central lines of the Underground system. The plans of British Railways for the terminus include redevelopment of the entire complex of the former London & North Western Railway goods depot, the North London Railway terminus and the former Great Eastern terminus. The North London Railway station is under-used and in the peaks the Great Eastern Railway line of the Eastern Region is hard-pressed by over seventy trains an hour at its eighteen platforms and six-track approach. A new railway hotel and new office block is included in the proposed commercial development, along with a bus station to replace the unsheltered street stands which are all that have been available for the waiting bus passenger for so many years. The terminating buses that wait in Liverpool Street outside Broad Street station have always been subject to harrying by the City of London police, being supposed to spend no more than two minutes setting down and picking up passengers. The North London Line Committee believes the North London will gain public attention from this rebuilding, in which its access on a viaduct will probably give it an elevated position.

Since the North London Line publication was issued, the official British Railway scheme for rebuilding Liverpool Street as a 22-platform station has been published. It would lie across the sites of Liverpool Street and Broad Street stations and North London trains would approach it from Richmond via the base of the Dalston triangle and a new connection from the North London to Poplar line and the Great Eastern Hackney Downs line north of London Fields. The Great Eastern might be widened to eight tracks (it is at present six) between Bethnal Green and Liverpool Street.

It is suggested by the North London Line Committee that the high concentration of population at the commercial and industrial centre of Shoreditch justifies the re-opening of Shoreditch station. Consideration for re-opening is the recommendation made in respect of Haggerston, Mildmay Park, and Maiden Lane, closures of 1940, 1934 and 1917 respectively. Reinstatement of Kentish Town West in Prince of Wales Road, is positively urged.

From Kentish Town West the Hampstead Junction section of the North London route swings up to Gospel Oak and Hampstead Heath, both in good residential districts, and then crosses to Finchley Road and Frognal across an area in which the North London trains provide a much more direct service than any of the local bus routes. In West

End Lane there is a remarkable series of stations, West Hampstead on the Metropolitan and Bakerloo Lines of London Transport, also passed through by British Rail trains from Marylebone to High Wycombe and Aylesbury, for which, however, there are no platforms. Almost opposite the Metropolitan Line station building is that of West End Lane (British Rail) served by the North London service. A few yards further north is West Hampstead British Rail station on the Midland line served by London Midland trains between St Pancras and Bedford. The Bakerloo trains of London Transport at West Hampstead are, of course, on the Stanmore service due to become an integral part of the Fleet Line. The North London Line Committee development pamphlet suggests that a comprehensive interchange station at this point would benefit all four railway routes concerned. What degree of integration of these stations on West End Lane is desirable obviously requires a degree of market research, but the improvement of ease of interchange of this sort nearly always generates new traffic.

Between Willesden Junction and Acton Central the North & South Western Junction Railway crosses the Central Line of London Transport, just east of the Central Line's station at North Acton where it splits for Ealing Broadway and West Ruislip. The North London Line Committee points out that an interchange station here would enable North London passengers to reach the projected Channel Tunnel White City terminal with only one stop at East Acton, or to change to the High Wycombe route by travelling westward via West Ruislip and the High Wycombe line, are also advocated in the proposal for a North Acton interchange.

From Gunnersbury the North London trains have a run of over a mile to Kew Gardens, and it is proposed that this should be divided at the point of crossing the London & South Western Railway Hounslow loop by a new station common to the North & South Western Junction and London & South Western Railway lines at Strand-on-the-Green; the station would be in a traffic-generating area at present not well served by other public transport media.

The North London Line Committee has thus put forward a scheme which is claimed to promote the further development of the North London at a fraction of the cost of various Outer Circle proposals. The NL scheme provides for interchange services to and from the North London at nine points, three of which are new, and a number of new or re-opened traffic-producing stations. There would be interchange with two London Transport Underground lines and the Eastern Region at Liverpool Street (new name for Broad Street), with the

Great Northern suburban electric lines of British Railways and London Transport Victoria Line at Highbury, with the British Rail St Pancras–Bedford service and facilities from Marylebone, and the London Transport Bakerloo and Metropolitan lines at West End Lane (renamed West Hampstead), with the British Rail services from Euston and the London Transport Bakerloo Line at Willesden Junction (there is a possibility of Bakerloo trains here all day when the car shed is established at Stonebridge Park), with the London Transport Central Line and British Rail services from Paddington at North Acton, with the London Transport District Line at Gunnersbury, with the British Rail Hounslow Loop service at Strand-on-the-Green, with the London Transport District service at Kew Gardens and with the District Line and British Rail services on the Southern Region at Richmond, where there are also, as at many other points, exceptionally good bus facilities.

It has been suggested on several occasions that the North London line should be handed over to London Transport for operation, much as under the 1935 plan several Great Northern and Great Eastern branches were taken over from the London & North Eastern Railway. The experiment of London Transport passenger operation and British Rail freight services does not seem to have been an undiluted success and it seems sighs of relief were uttered when the closing of local goods depots rendered the arrangement no longer necessary. London Transport operating really requires that undertaking's distinctive signalling, trip stops (the stock of steam locomotives fitted for working on London Transport lines was a hampering factor in operation) and segregated tracks, while commercial methods call for a denser train service than British Rail finds economic and a coarsely-zoned fare scale.

A compromise proposal is that the North London should appear on London Transport maps and literature so that it is brought to the attention of visitors to the Metropolis along with Underground facilities. Segregation of tracks would call for the Hampstead Junction line to be omitted from British Rail freight routing, re-opening of the four North London tracks where they have been given up, and difficult decisions to be made about the North & South Western Junction line from near Willesden Junction to south of Acton Central, a section over which, even if there were space, the laying of additional tracks would not be an inviting proposition economically. Part of the North London freight business, from Willesden to Victoria Park, and thence over the former Great Eastern tracks to Temple Mills, is in any event subject to consideration for 25kv electrification with overhead conductor wires.

The value of the gains to be obtained by transfer of the North London Line to London Transport or inclusion on that undertaking's publicity is still to be assessed; there are already distinctive British Railway poster maps portraying the advantages of circling the northern suburbs on North London trains. One of the evils to be overcome is vandalism; this has in the past destroyed one station completely and reduced the amenities at others. Evening trains of three cars run with the doors locked on the middle coach, so that the coaches used by passengers are under the supervision either of the driver or the guard. Where stations have been rebuilt, as the platforms at Willesden Junction High Level or Gospel Oak, the British Railway architects' department has achieved pleasing and modern results.

six

RING
RAIL

Many people have turned their thoughts to greater use of existing railways when confronted by the absurdities created by the vogue of the motor car. The motor car as a means of rush-hour commuter transport conveys perhaps 10 per cent of the traffic mainly by cars in which the driver alone is being carried; immense congestion is thus caused by vehicles taking up 64 per cent of the road space, whereas buses carry 15 per cent of the commuters for an occupancy of 1·3 per cent of the road space. Apart from staff difficulties the bus is actually severely penalised by the flood of car traffic, yet the irregularities of bus service thus caused are always proclaimed by the advocates of the polluting car transport. Means of alleviating traffic congestion involve destruction of swathes of housing and involve the unattractive cityscapes of many American cities where all has been sacrificed to the great god Motor, as Hamilton Ellis, the evocative railway writer, has called it.

Out of thoughts turning towards better employment of the London railway system it is perhaps not surprising that the aims sought over a century ago and many times since by an Outer Circle system have been looked at again. In 1973 the encirclement of London by rail was again propounded, after a couple of years of study, by G. L. Crowther, P. H. Vickers and A. D. Pilling in *A New Ring Rail for London*, published by Just & Co. Ltd, 71 New Oxford Street, London, WC1A 1DN, which elaborates a possible means of accomplishing this purpose and its hoped-for advantages. The idea is set out for testing and, indeed, the proposal is one that should be investigated, even though it is difficult to accept that what was thought unsuitable for London and a diversion of capital expenditure into the wrong channels in 1864, subsequently would not be, in the belt-tightening times of 1975, still counted as contributing but little to the mobility of the Metropolis.

The authors suggest that the Ring Rail they propose, at the radius of Willesden, Clapham, Lewisham and Stratford, would sufficiently ease the inner London transport burden to dispense with the need for an inner motorway ring. It is intended to improve the transport of passengers and freight both within and through London by providing an orbital route additional to the Circle Line of London Transport, by interchange stations between Ring Rail and British Railways and London Transport radial routes, at which all main-line trains would stop; part of the value would be derived by a frequent and punctual service on Ring Rail and a fare structure to encourage its use. The interchanges, it is suggested, should be sited so that they are highly suitable for urban development and specimen layouts are included. The cost of the Ring Rail proposed was put at £200 million in 1973, compared with at least £1,000 million for the inner motorway box, and it is thought that a privately financed consortium could take on the provision of Ring Rail.

Beginning at Willesden Junction, an interchange station would be provided there with the London Midland main line from Euston to the North-West and Scotland. Ring Rail would then use the West London and West London Extension Railways. At Mitre Bridge, the crossing of the Western Region main line from Paddington would have another interchange station. A station would be provided at White City in the Crowther–Vickers–Pilling plan, but the map merely records that this is close to the BBC Television Centre and makes no reference to the possibilities of serving the projected British Railways Channel Tunnel terminal; mention is made of the scheme put forward by the GLC and rejected by British Railways for a Channel Tunnel terminal on the Surrey Docks site. The interchange is styled Latimer Road and the thought in *A New Ring Rail for London* is simply of interchange with the Hammersmith & City section of the Metropolitan. A Shepherd's Bush interchange is contemplated with the Central Line Uxbridge Road station. Going on to the West London Extension Railway an interchange is proposed at Earl's Court West to provide for passengers using the District Line to Ealing and Richmond and the Piccadilly Line to Uxbridge, and, of more importance, Hounslow and Heathrow for London Airport. This would involve a new station site for the District on an awkward curve and a new deep-level station on the Piccadilly Line a few yards west of the existing Earl's Court station. A further interchange of passengers with the District Wimbledon Line would take place at West Brompton.

Still using the West London Extension Railway, Ring Rail would turn towards the former London, Chatham & Dover and London, Brighton & South Coast Railways' South London line and in doing so pass under the London & South Western main line of the Southern Region. Here

an elaborate new £20 million interchange is advocated with four tracks
on the Ring Rail lines and two platforms from which there would be in
all 20 vertical links to the 22 main-line platforms proposed. It is a little
difficult to understand why so many platforms are considered necessary
because it is to deal basically with the traffic on three four-track main
lines – the London & South Western Railway Windsor lines, the London & South Western Railway main line and the London, Brighton &
South Coast Railway main line. It is thought that the time is ripe for
the redevelopment of the Clapham Junction area and that the importance of the Ring Rail project justifies the destruction of the small
number of houses on the new station site, which would in fact be at the
foot of the slope used by Brighton line trains between Victoria and
Battersea Park and Clapham Junction, at Pouparts Junction. If one
takes the diagram of the New Clapham Junction interchange literally,
it appears that the former Nine Elms freight tracks are to be given
passenger platforms on the north side of the station and that the low-
level approach to Victoria via Stewarts Lane box and the link from the
West London Extension to South Lambeth goods depot are to be
reduced to a single track.

Another course of action for the Clapham Junction interchange
leaves that station on its present site and approaches it for Ring Rail
purposes in a terminal tunnel which would have low-level platforms
below the existing surface station. Manifestly this would not be so
satisfactory from the viewpoint of Ring Rail operation and would need
over a mile of new tunnel at an estimated cost in 1973 of £16 million.
As this so closely approaches the estimate for removal of the interchange to a point almost three-quarters of a mile to the east it would
obviously be a matter for close examination if the scheme were adopted
and could presumably be resolved on the score of convenience rather
than cost. The advocates of Ring Rail suggest in any event that the new
station here would 'be a rewarding challenge to architects to transform
that image of bleak and anonymous platforms into a bright and cheerful
interchange'.

Between the new Clapham Junction and the new interchange at
Clapham the tracks of Ring Rail change direction to follow the South
London Line from Factory Junction. The Clapham interchange, close
to the site of Clapham (earlier Clapham Road) on the South London
line and of the long-closed platforms on the London, Chatham & Dover
tracks, would enable a connection by escalator to be made with the
Northern Line of London Transport. At Brixton a link between Ring
Rail and the London Transport Victoria Line is proposed for

passengers. Further along the South London line Loughborough
Junction on the radial routes from Holborn Viaduct would be selected
for the East Brixton interchange, linking Ring Rail to services from
the City to outer suburban Kent. This new station, east of the
present East Brixton stop for South London line trains, occurs at
a point where both lines are on viaduct, so that it would involve costly
construction.

Next interchange point selected by Crowther, Pilling and Vickers is
Peckham Rye and the cost of alterations between Peckham Rye and
Nunhead is put at £9 million. This is one of the places where lack of
knowledge of everyday railway working appears to let the authors down.
They suggest that Ring Rail trains could be turned from the southern
to the northern pair of tracks west of Peckham Rye and could then
proceed eastward through Nunhead to the rest of Ring Rail. The
authors proceed:

> Three radial services and the Continental services would then
> be diverted through Brixton, Herne Hill, Sydenham Hill to
> Bromley South and points beyond. The argument here is that
> if four services can use only two tracks from Victoria to
> Brixton they can use two as far as Shortlands.

It is recognised that the disruption of existing services would be high,
and a local shuttle service from Bromley South to Nunhead would do
little to mitigate the inconvenience for passengers at Bellingham, Catford and Crofton Park, to name only three stations on the Catford
Loop. But what does not seem to be clear in the minds of the authors is
that from Brixton to Shortlands the existing two two-track railways are
used as four tracks. There are local radial services from Victoria via
Sydenham Hill to Bromley South and Orpington, from Victoria in the
peaks to Kent House, and from Holborn in the peaks via Sydenham
Hill to Bromley South and beyond as well as all day from Holborn to
Nunhead, Catford, Bromley South and the Sevenoaks line. But besides
the bulk of Continental services which run via Sydenham Hill (and not
as assumed in *A New Ring Rail for London* via Nunhead and Catford)
there is a very heavy service of trains making the first stop from Victoria
or the City at Bromley South, *en route* to Gillingham, Maidstone,
Ashford and beyond, the Thanet resorts, Dover via Canterbury or
Sheerness. These run not only via Sydenham Hill, but also via Catford
and the operation of the local services from Victoria and Holborn
depends on use of the route via Catford as well as that via Sydenham
Hill by these trains. For example a local train may leave Victoria at 12

minutes past the hour and is followed by a non-stop to Bromley South at 14 minutes past. The latter is not delayed by the all-stations train because it diverges at Brixton to run via Catford at a time when there is a gap between local trains calling at stations on the Catford Loop. It is difficult to see why the authors considered this important main line via Sydenham Hill would need 'up-grading', as they advocate in Appendix F. The glib solution of the Peckham Rye interchange problem put forward first therefore seems impossible to accept.

Recourse to the second and more complicated solution would there-fore be necessary with provision of extra tracks at a different level between a point west of the bifurcation of the Sutton line from the South London line west of Peckham Rye and somewhere east of the departure of the Catford Loop from the alignment of the original London, Chatham & Dover Greenwich Park branch. The Ring Rail tracks might have to be separated vertically from the former London, Chatham & Dover lines by a considerable distance, as from Peckham Rye to Nunhead the existing railway is on a viaduct high above the surrounding street pattern. It is suggested that at Peckham Rye the Ring Rail platforms could be fitted into the gap between the platforms used by Eastern and Central Division (ex-LC&DR and LBSC) ser-vices, but a more fundamental rearrangement providing for cross-platform exchanges of passengers might be desirable.

The essay on Ring Rail takes it from Nunhead over the former Lon-don, Chatham & Dover Greenwich Park branch (now used by freight *en route* to Kent and for a limited commuter service in peak hours between Dartford and Holborn via Bexleyheath and the line via Sidcup formerly known as the Dartford Loop line) to an interchange with the London, Brighton & South Coast main line from London Bridge to Croydon and Brighton at Brockley. Another interchange is proposed at St John's with the South Eastern main line from Charing Cross to Tonbridge and Dover. This is complicated; since Messrs Crowther, Vickers and Pilling made their study the Southern Region has embarked on construction of a flyover from the Lewisham loop crossing of the main line to the fast track side of the main line to enable acceleration of trains between the Dartford area and the London termini. This is being carried out in conjunction with the alterations between New Cross and London Bridge that will make possible removal of the conflicting movements at the point of bifurcation to Cannon Street from the Charing Cross route—the notorious Borough Market Junction which nevertheless has been, over half a century of electric train operation, a monument to railway efficiency and the skill and enterprise of successive generations of signalmen. To fit the interchange in, the entire reconstruction of existing railways in the St John's and Lewisham Junction area would have to be undertaken.

From St John's alternative proposals are made for Ring Rail: One route, not surveyed by the authors, would have the virtue of shortening the whole circuit to 28 miles instead of 29¼ and would take it to Greenwich (interchange with the Southern Region Woolwich line) and, passing under the Thames, through what is recognised as a problem area on the Isle of Dogs to the North London line at Poplar. On the North London line there would be an interchange at Bromley-by-Bow with the London Transport District Line to Upminster and the LTS line to Tilbury and Southend, involving a displacement westward of the present Bromley-by-Bow station, interchange with the Great Eastern main line to the Eastern Counties via Ipswich at Bow (new station sites on both lines). Thence Ring Rail would go on to Hackney Wick (the site of Victoria Park station) where it rejoins the scheme more definitely put forward for this eastern section of Ring Rail. The Bromley-by-Bow and Bow interchanges would involve entirely new station construction on new and constricted sites.

The main suggestion for the eastern sector involves a difficult sharing of the two-track Southern Suburban line from St John's as far as Blackheath. It is proposed that the Dartford via Blackheath and Woolwich service be abandoned and that in the interests of Ring Rail the Fleet Line be extended from New Cross direct to Blackheath via a new Greenwich South, or as planned via Lewisham to Blackheath, with extension thence along the Bexleyheath line to Dartford. Another possible course would be to four-track the section between the St John's interchange and Blackheath to provide accommodation for both services. In the present writer's opinion this would be the preferable line to take, since replacement of the Southern mix of eight- and ten-car trains on the Bexleyheath line at the rate of 10 or 11 in the peak hour (giving more than 11,500 seats in the hour) by 30 or so Fleet Line tube trains (with perhaps only 9,000 seats) would not be appreciated by the inhabitants of Bexleyheath and Barnehurst. There is also a difficulty in accommodating the greatly increased service on the two-track approach to the proposed terminal of the service at Dartford, used also by Southern trains *en route* to Dartford via three other routes and including a proportion of trains for Gravesend, Gillingham and Maidstone, and beyond.

The complications of installing London Transport signalling and automatic operation over a section of track used by trains of alien type are too great for contemplation as the Fleet Line is intended to be operated with one-man trains similarly to the Victoria Line.

To resume the Ring Rail proposals, an interchange station is proposed at Westcombe Park, resited to provide connection for Ring Rail passengers with the Woolwich and Erith (or North Kent) line of the Southern. From there it would run by a mile-long tunnel under the River Thames to Canning Town, for which detailed proposals have been published. Twin 20 ft outside diameter bores are proposed, to be 45 ft maximum depth under the river. The planned gradient over a ⅞-mile descent from Westcombe Park is 1 in 102 and on the ¾-mile northern slope, 1 in 88. The depth of the river bed at the Angerstein Tunnel is stated to be 20 or 22 ft maximum. This alignment for a tunnel was adumbrated in the Railway Plan for London and the subsequent Working Party Report of 1949. Ring Rail in this version of the eastern sector would join the former Great Eastern North Woolwich branch just south of Canning Town where there would be an interchange for North Woolwich line passengers. On this trace the interchange with the LTS line would be at West Ham, just west of the present West Ham District station, and the interchange with the Great Eastern in the Stratford complex in the position of the Stratford Low Level platforms. This would have the benefit of providing a connection with the Central Line as well.

At Victoria Park, or Hackney Wick as the Ring Rail calls it to define the district served more closely, with a name made familiar over many years as a bus service destination, the alternative eastern sectors of Ring Rail unite to continue over the North London and Hampstead Junction lines to Willesden Junction. Hackney Wick is listed as an interchange with the Poplar line; next comes Hackney Downs interchange where passengers could be exchanged with the services from Liverpool Street to Enfield, the Hertford and Cambridge lines and Chingford. The station, remote from the shopping area, would not serve the same local purposes as the Hackney station of the London Transport SW–NE Line. Highbury would be an important interchange between Ring Rail and the former Great Northern & City Railway, soon to be carrying Great Northern line suburban trains of British Railways. It would also serve the Victoria Line *en route* from Walthamstow to Brixton. Another interchange would be placed at Vale Royal, where the North London crosses the Great Northern main line out of King's Cross on the high viaduct that gave trouble in 1850. The authors of *A New Ring Rail for London* consider that a new Piccadilly Line station should be made here for the interchange, which is just north of the York Road station closed in 1932.

[88]

Camden is another interchange deemed important by the authors of *A New Ring Rail for London*. It would make a link with the Northern Line tube of London Transport. The physical difficulties would be considerable, since the North London Line crosses Camden Road the best part of a quarter-mile from the junction of Camden Road and Camden High Street, where the tube station entrance is placed. It is nearly as far up Kentish Town Road to the point where the Hampstead Junction line leaves the North London. Most of the differences could be overcome by escalators or moving walkways, of course, if it were deemed a vital matter. But the authors of *A New Ring Rail for London* think that the Hampstead branch of the Northern Line should be diverted to effect this interchange, and the cost of a rearrangement of the Northern Line Camden Town junctions and new twin-tube tunnel from the new interchange station to Chalk Farm gets no special mention in the list of estimates.

It is proposed to close the present Gospel Oak and replace it with an interchange station a little to the south, between Ring Rail on the Hampstead Junction line at the point where it crosses the connection from the Midland main line to the Tottenham & Hampstead line; and provision is made in the diagram reproduced in the book for a station to deal with trains from Maplin airport; that scheme had not been abandoned, of course, when the book on Ring Rail was published. Trains over the Tottenham & Forest Gate line from Barking would use this interchange and no longer run to St Pancras in the view of the authors of this book.

Considerable attention is given to the next interchange, at West Hampstead, for which a cost of £2 million is allocated. As the book says, within a distance of 200 yards along West End Lane three stations already exist. 'This is a unique site for the bold and imaginative planning of a new interchange station.' Lines from Marylebone (ex-GCR), Baker Street (Metropolitan and Fleet), St Pancras (ex-Midland) and the Ring Rail (ex-Hampstead Junction) come so close together, with six platforms in use, that it seems an opportunity for a much grander twelve-platform station providing opportunity for passengers from Leicester, Luton, Aylesbury and High Wycombe to change to the outer London circuit instead of going direct to a central London terminus. The physical means of establishing 'West Hampstead Twelve Ways', whether by moving walkways or by fundamental diversions of existing routes are not defined in a diagram on page 66 of the book, but it would probably be very costly to make this interchange effective, since the Hampstead Junction line lies at an angle, crossing from the north side of the Midland route to the south side of the Metropolitan over a distance of about half a mile. Any provision of cross-platform exchanges of passengers over what were shown to be the most favoured routes would involve much change of level and new construction of diversionary formations for the new alignments of the tracks. Only prolonged investigation and an extensive travel census would reveal the need for any particular arrangement of the platforms as compared with other possible arrangements. A diagram, Figure 18, however, shows the West Hampstead proposal as an integrated station with ten parallel platform faces for the four-track Midland and six-track Metropolitan, Fleet and Great Central lines and with the two Hampstead Junction tracks crossing roughly at right angles. To avoid use of the existing stations between West Hampstead and Willesden a 'fully integrated' local bus route over this section could be provided or, as diagram 18 shows, what the authors term a 'cab track' with new stops added to those on the Hampstead Junction. This is otherwise undefined suspended railway on which work by the Transport and Road Research Laboratory and the Department of the Environment ceased some time ago.

At Willesden Junction the authors of *A New Ring Rail for London* suggest a linking at high level of the Hampstead Junction line from West Hampstead with the West London line to Clapham Junction and either abandonment of the North & South Western Junction line to Gunnersbury and Richmond, or provision of a terminal track alongside the Ring Rail tracks. It is also suggested that passenger service on the North & South Western Junction could be abandoned. New platforms would be required to provide interchange with the main-line services from Euston to the North-West and Scotland.

Although, like all the other Outer Circle schemes that have ever been propounded, Ring Rail has some obvious attractions and the authors go into much detail, from provision of next train indicators on platforms, and general layout of stations, to the type of rolling stock that should be provided, little is said to show that the disruption of existing arrangements that would be caused has been taken into account. On the freight side, it is true, a London bypass is advocated, a little like that considered by the Railway Executive roundly a quarter-century ago, and beginning or ending at Redhill with a viaduct direct from the Guildford to the Tonbridge direction across the London to Brighton route, but proceeding north from Oxford to Birmingham. Another London avoiding route shown on a map, from Harwich via Peterborough to the North and Midlands, is, of course, the route that the London & North Eastern Railway catered for when Whitemoor marshalling yard for Eastern Counties traffic was built at March in 1929. Three other possibilities are suggested for traffic that does use Ring Rail routes: night operation; day freight trains capable of keeping pace with Ring Rail passenger service; and day operation into long freight service loops which would enable the Ring Rail service to continue uninterrupted.

The main objection to Ring Rail is probably the question of whether it would be used sufficiently to justify the expenditure and the frequent services proposed, which are no doubt vital to make it worth the while of any passenger to go the great way round. For this is a human feeling that applies particularly to the taking of unnecessarily long journeys, and acutely to those that have to be paid for by mileage. From time to time British Railways policy has been to make the passenger pay for every yard he travels, whether he is suiting his own convenience or not by taking a longer route and there is no foreseeing whether at some time it would not become British Railways policy in respect of Ring Rail, no matter what inducements to use it were dangled before the traveller in the initial stages. As to whether people would ever willingly go round a circle to reach their destination one has only to study the short cuts across the Inner Circle railways, especially the use of the 36 bus from Victoria to Paddington, despite congestion in Park Lane, to sense the reluctance of the average citizen to go the long way round, even if it is the 'shortest way home' in terms of time. Study of winding paved paths in a hundred spots from the campus of Loughborough University to an indirect path to a public lavatory in the Library Gardens, Bromley, shows graphically, by the trampling of beautifully laid lawns into muddy paths that human beings have a great revulsion to circuitous routes. So the present writer is sceptical of benefits of the Ring Rail proposal, although not averse to a further investigation, perhaps with a census of rail and other passengers' needs similar to the comprehensive survey of what Southern Region passengers wanted in the way of train services before the great timetable reforms of 1967.

The other point about Ring Rail that would need much thought and patient research is how it would affect Inter City services. Would they gain traffic from the presence of Ring Rail or would the irritation of a stop just as one was settling to a long fast journey be so much as to reduce custom? Some of the Ring Rail interchanges would insert a stop in services which have long had a tradition of a fast run out of London; others would add the burden of a second stop because the Watford or other outer London stop has become an essential part of the operating pattern. At Vale Royal, by the chance of the location of the North London tracks, main-line trains from King's Cross would be halted a little over half a mile from the platform ends of the terminus to exchange passengers with Ring Rail trains. At all these interchanges, if Ring Rail succeeded in attracting large numbers of passengers those joining long-distance expresses would have the discomfort of forcing their way into already crowded trains, unless block seat reservations for Ring Rail passengers were provided.

seven

FREIGHT ACROSS LONDON

Fears expressed by the pundits of 1846 about street traffic congestion in the centre of London were, of course, rendered only too true by the ring of separate main-line termini decreed by Parliament and only alleviated to a limited degree by the connections between main lines effected by the North London, North & South Western Junction, West London Extension, the Metropolitan Widened Lines and London, Chatham & Dover link, the Tottenham & Hampstead Junction and East London Railways.

Despite pious hopes most of these remained very inefficient as railways owing to steep gradients, sharp curvature and limited lengths of train in block sections, between stop signals and protective catch points or in refuge sidings. The East London Railway, for example, included several gradients of 1 in 40 in tunnel and where steam engines on freight trains had to condense, the entry from the Great Eastern Railway was by running into the terminal platforms at Liverpool Street and reversing (putting a 26-wagon limit on train length in any event) or by means of a hoist at Spitalfields, installed in 1900, which took 10-ton wagons two at a time to and from sidings installed at the Great Eastern depot and the tracks laid in an abortive branch of the East London designed originally to give that railway an outlet to the Great Eastern at Cambridge Heath, but never completed owing to the abysmal state of East London finances.

The Tottenham & Hampstead line, also laid out by an impecunious and speculative company, included a 1 in 48 bank up from the Midland Railway, and a long 1 in 97 through Harringay Park. It led to the Tottenham & Forest Gate Railway (joint Midland and London, Tilbury & Southend) of 1894 which went on to viaduct between Walthamstow and Leyton Midland Road on a 1 in 64 bank and came from it at Wanstead Park by a 1 in 65 gradient into cutting at Woodgrange Park on its way to Barking. The connections to the Metropolitan Widened Lines included a 1 in 58 gradient from the Midland at St Paul's Road

[94]

and 1 in 46 falling from York Road on the Great Northern Line and
1 in 48 on a sharp curve climbing to the Great Northern (the 'hotel
curve' at King's Cross) together with a section at 1 in 40 after passing
under the Metropolitan's original line at Farringdon Street and a 1 in
39 on the slope up through Snow Hill to the heights of the London,
Chatham & Dover viaduct over Ludgate Hill. For many years goods
trains on the Widened Lines were restricted to 23 wagons, but as
recently as 1950 the limit was relaxed to 32 wagons. The length of
sidings at Temple Mills, Acton and Brent yards kept the length of other
trains handling interchange traffic to 44 or 49 wagons according to
circumstances. After the traffic reached the Southern, the route to
Norwood yards, for example, involved negotiation of severe gradients,
especially on the Clapham Junction to Crystal Palace section where the
former West End of London & Crystal Palace Railway was on a course
across hilly country necessitating inclines as steep as 1 in 70.

A move for amelioration of rail freight traffic exchange came from
an unexpected quarter in about 1910 when A. Warwick Gattie, a bank
official, began lecturing on the benefits of container transport and a
freight clearing house which, he suggested, should be built on a 30-
acre site between Goswell Road and St John Street. Ignoring the coal
traffic then such a high proportion of the freight handled at London's
seventy-four goods stations, Gattie proposed a twenty-four-track depot
to replace them and rapid transfer of containers from railway wagon to
lorry and vice versa. To accord with the then capabilities of motor
transport 3-ton lorries and correspondingly small containers were proposed; later sights were lifted somewhat and 5-ton lorries were specified.
The movement of trains on new tunnel railways by electric traction
from King's Cross (Great Western, Great Northern and Midland),
Bishopsgate (Great Eastern), and Snow Hill (London, Chatham &
Dover) would have given access to all the main lines centred on London
and seems easier to visualise than the street traffic generated by 5,000
comparatively small lorries which coarse statistics assembled by Gattie
sought to show would have *reduced* street traffic in the central area.
There were several inquiries into this scheme, notably a Board of Trade
departmental investigation in 1919.

Unfortunately Gattie, although he had the root of the matter in him
and had devised a transfer system of great ingenuity for sorting small
containers to a variety of destinations, and conceived container shipping
equipment not dissimilar from the aspect of a modern container port, was
quite incapable of a lucid explanation of his system; his chosen publicist,
Roy Horniman, gave a no less confused account in *How to Make the*

Railways Pay for the War in 1919. Probably the first clear account of the proposed working of the Gattie system was by David R. Lamb, a former Great Central Railway officer, in the pages of the weekly technical newspaper *Modern Transport* in the summer of that year. The Departmental Committee made its report on its investigations in 1919 and decided very much against the proposals of the New Transport Co. Ltd and Gattie; Warwick Gattie was run over by a boy on a bicycle in 1925 and broke an arm; unfortunately complications set in and his death resulted. In 1927 the four grouped railways adopted their scheme for road and rail conveyance of containers of 2- to 4-ton capacity; by 1950 British Railways had the largest stock of containers of reasonable size (many Continental containers were only of one cubic metre capacity) of any country in Western Europe. Since 1965 British Railways has been able to implement the Freightliner method of container handling and in this has once more been ahead of the railways of the Continent west of the Iron Curtain.

Nevertheless this is one of the factors that has greatly simplified working on British Railways and so reduced the flow of wagons across London. When the improvement of cross-London freight facilities was considered again after the 1930 investigation of an 'outer circle' link across the northern circumference of London, it was in the light of wartime stresses in the aftermath of the so-called Abercrombie Report (drawn up by J. H. Forshaw, architect to the London County Council, in association with Professor (later Sir) Patrick Abercrombie). This was successor to one of the grandiose post-war reconstruction schemes popular in 1943 and in this case issued in pamphlet form by the London Regional Reconstruction Committee of the Royal Institute of British Architects. A combined northern terminus was to be provided to replace Euston, St Pancras and King's Cross. Although Paddington and Liverpool Street were to be allowed to survive, all the Southern termini were to be swept away to be replaced by a unified Southern terminal. All the terminal stations would have incorporated loops on which the suburban services would have reversed. A new Inner Circle, diverting to the south side of the river to serve the Southern terminus, would have supplanted the old and a revival of the 1864 Metropolitan District scheme would have provided an Outer Circle over a very similar route including Clapham Junction and Bow. Estimates of cost were pointedly omitted.

Almost naturally the Abercrombie Report was a mixed bag of architectural idealism which had as solution to London's problems the driving of railways from the surface to deep-level underground routes and their replacement by a network of viaduct roads which it was claimed would not be so divisive of neighbourhoods – a matter of opinion for which no evidence was offered. The railway features of Abercrombie were examined by the Ministry of Transport Railway (London Plan) Committee, 1944, and then by the British Transport Commission London Plan Working Party, 1948.

At that time it was thought that early removal of Blackfriars railway bridge (the first section of which was built in 1864) would be necessitated by town planning requirements and would thus bring freight traffic on the Widened Lines to an end. A new freight route in tunnel was therefore proposed from Loughborough Junction to Farringdon Street. Another route was also proposed, also by under-river tunnel, from Hither Green marshalling yard to Canning Town by Lewisham Junction and East Greenwich. A link to the Great Eastern was thus the primary objective, but a connection to the North London near Bow and via both the Great Eastern and North London routes to the Great Northern, Midland and London & North Western systems, would also have been provided. Better curvature and gradients throughout, thus avoiding some of the defects that even with the Loughborough–Farringdon tunnel would have attached to the Widened Lines, as well as a connection to the London, Tilbury & Southend line without involving crossing the District electrified lines alongside the London, Tilbury & Southend tracks (not yet segregated), would have been achieved. The Greenwich sub-Thames tunnel would have made possible 40-wagon trains and so improved cross-London freight working. It would also have enabled the closing of the East London as a freight route, in addition to the elimination of the Widened Lines and Blackfriars crossing of the central area. The cost would, however, at 1949 prices, have been at least £5 million more than the Loughborough–Farringdon tunnel. But the possibility of greater ease of cross-London freight working and better facilities for through passenger services were recognised, although careful analysis of prospective traffic was thought desirable before any commitment was made.

Indeed, recognition of the immense cost of, and lack of sufficient remunerative traffic for, the tunnel link between Loughborough and Farringdon was made very early in the 1950s and explains the subsequent lack of interest in the fundamental redevelopment of the route as a modern tunnel railway for the freight trains of the latter part of the century; the likely changes in operating techniques and traffic volume were also recognised although published statements were somewhat vague.

[97]

By 1951 the steam had gone out of the Greenwich proposal and the removal of Blackfriars railway bridge had ceased to be a cardinal point with the town planners. Probably by that time the fall in domestic fuel traffic to South London was already ceasing to make operation of some seventy trains of twenty-plus wagons per train over the Widened Lines and Blackfriars route a paramount feature of London freight working. The affluent society with liquid fuel, gas or electric central heating, had doomed the huge pre-1939 volume of coal traffic to reduction if not extinction and this was accompanied by a swing towards road transport for general freight and even at some times and on some routes for coal class traffic.

As a result of the reduction of traffic volume and other rationalisation of railway freight traffic, it has been possible to reduce the number of cross-London freight routes, two having been given up in the quarter-century since nationalisation. Formation of British Railways has enabled adoption of new routing strategies which even between 1971 and 1974 have reduced inter-regional wagon transfer in the Metropolis from a daily average of 3,983 to 3,271. Movement to and from the Southern Region has fallen from 11,000 wagons a day in 1950 to fewer than 2,000 a quarter-century later.

On the East London route closure had been unavoidable at certain periods during the Second World War, when the West London Railway had been used instead; after 17 April 1966, when the line between East London Junction on the Great Eastern and Shoreditch station on the East London was closed, the arrangement became permanent. The Spitalfields hoist, which came into provisional operation on 11 June 1900 and regular use from 1 October of that year would in any event have been affected by the disastrous fire at Spitalfields depot which brought about its closure from 6 November 1967.

Outlets from the Widened Lines route gradually diminished in number; even Walworth Road Midland coal depot, which was being reconstructed for about eighteen months in 1958–9, was later closed completely.

The Great Northern coal depot at Elephant and Castle was shut on 1 July 1863. The Midland was most energetic of the companies to open coal depots on other railways, probably the most extreme example, over 40 miles from its own tracks, being the depot at Maidstone on the London, Chatham & Dover, for which authority was obtained from Parliament on 3 July 1884. This had long been given up, but the Brixton depot was only closed in the last days of the London, Midland & Scottish, in 1947.

For its own depots the Southern Region planned a drastic reduction; some of the survivors, such as Beckenham Junction, no longer cater for any general freight, but are in use as coal concentration depots only, in which capacity traffic consists largely of block trains. Miscellaneous freight and small traffic is concentrated on depots such as Bricklayers' Arms, distribution being by road vehicle, nowadays of National Carriers. The closure process was carried out in an apparently haphazard manner; to take a selection of Mid-Kent line goods yards, Catford Bridge was closed 23 March 1968; Lower Sydenham on 20 June 1966; Clock House on 19 April 1965; Elmers End on 6 May 1963; West Wickham on 2 September 1963; Hayes on 19 April 1965; Woodside on 30 September 1963; and Addiscombe on 17 June 1968. There is no easily discernible pattern, but it is fairly safe to say that all wayside depots on the South Eastern & Chatham section of the Southern were closed during the 1960s.

Closure of the Widened Lines and Blackfriars Bridge freight route took place over a long period. The old Blackfriars Bridge was progressively closed after 1960, by which time it was becoming almost a centenarian. The last trains over the Blackfriars to West Street route (junction with the Metropolitan) was a Southern Region parcel train which ran on 23 March 1969. The closing took place on the next day after which no regular traffic passed. Complete closure took place on 3 May 1971. No traffic has passed over the old Blackfriars Bridge since 27 June 1971. Final stage was the taking out of the junctions with the Metropolitan, making operation between the Southern Region and the Widened Lines no longer possible.

In the meantime one of the committees of which the British Transport Commission and the Railway Executive were excessively enamoured sat in the early 1950s to examine cross-London freight operation; they did not consider the traffic of those days could be handled effectively by a limited selection of the existing routes, but advocated an entirely new and roundabout channel for north–south traffic.

Development of suburban services and the probable need of new marshalling yards to be located further out than Temple Mills, Ferme Park, Brent and Willesden, with the then gloomy prognostications of the difficulties of handling continuous-braked freight trains in yards, and a realisation of the need of replanning freight services as a whole, led to the new thought on the subject, leading to greater economy of scarce capital resources. It was felt to be more realistic to provide a new main-line route round London – a sort of revival of the hoary Outer Circle project – even though on a route from north to south involving much longer mileage for such transfer. The route chosen called for no extensive provision of new lines and it was thought effective relief to the problems posed would be attained for a modest outlay of capital, and could be carried out quicker than any of the fundamental solutions involving sub-aqueous tunnels.

The proposal was simply to convert the under-used Cambridge–Sandy–Bedford–Bletchley–Calvert–Oxford line into a freight trunk route which would give access from all the northern trunk routes to the Western Region Oxford–Didcot–Reading line and thence to the Southern Region Reading–Guildford–Redhill line. By avoiding central London problems of commuter routes and congested marshalling yards would be solved; the coal class, heavy freight and much general merchandise would be taken out of the central maelstrom, together with the related empty wagon mileage, and effect automatic improvement on the conditions in the London area.

The point has to be made that since Beeching some of the railways concerned have been abandoned and the former roadbeds diverted to other uses. Greater London Council housing developments have effectively blocked the whole route from Sandy to Bedford, for example.

The route advocated in the early 1950s made a convenient junction with the former Great Eastern system at Cambridge and there followed 21 miles of double track to Sandy, with 4 miles of rising line, mainly at 1 in 100 and 1 in 105, to Gamlingay and almost 2 miles down at 1 in 150 towards Potton. At Sandy there was a difficult goods yard connection with the Great Northern main line and a war-time running junction from north to west. The bridge over the Great Northern main line limited the size of locomotive to Class 6F, but only two additional east-bound trains were proposed for this section.

From Sandy westward to Bedford was 8¾ miles of single track. At Bedford the link with the Midland main line was even more difficult than that with the Great Northern at Sandy and would have involved suspension of goods yard operation in the Midland depot when transfers were taking place. The Hitchin branch of the Midland is crossed on the level. From Sandy to Oxford Class 8F freight locomotives could be employed. Between Bedford and Bletchley the ruling gradient over 3 miles of the 16 was 1 in 129, with a limit of 59 wagons on an 8F engine and 29 on a 2F, whereas the length limit imposed by track and signalling considerations was 70 wagons. At Bletchley the London & North Western main line was crossed on the level.

The Bletchley–Oxford stretch included a 4-mile bank on the way to Swanbourne with gradients of 1 in 150 and 1 in 142. Only a Class 8 freight engine could be rostered on a 66-wagon train, but the physical limit of train length was 60 wagons. There was a nest of eleven sorting sidings at Swanbourne, the shunting neck for which was limited to accommodating 60 wagons. Something like 2,400 wagons of coal class traffic and empties could have been diverted to this route daily.

New works were required for handling this volume of traffic by the new route: a double-track link from north to west to obtain traffic from the Midland main line at Bedford; a flyover at Bletchley to avoid conflicting movements across the London & North Western Railway main line from Euston and an improved layout for the station, which had not in the 1950s attained the status of a station for the new town of Milton Keynes. As the Great Central main-line closure was not then an issue a junction for east to south traffic with the Great Central route was proposed at Calvert. At Swanbourne, the existing sidings were, it was proposed, to be developed into a full-scale Calvert marshalling yard where trains could be sorted into the order required for their points of destination on the Western and Southern Regions. This would enable elimination of smaller yards on those regions and of tripping movements between them. The Western Region would have received a few trains for London via the Great Western & Great Central Joint Line and a series of trains from the Calvert yard for distribution in the south-west. This would have increased Oxford–Didcot traffic by 14 trains one way and 21 the other, and new works were expected to be necessitated by this, as a suggestion for a very limited through passenger service from Norwich to Bristol, made by that very discerning railway thinker, G. F. Fiennes, had been turned down shortly before on the score of congestion at Oxford.

A wry reflection on the railway system before Beeching is that it was contemplated at this time that some of the traffic to Southern Region destinations should go via Didcot, Newbury and Winchester. After Reading over 600 wagons a day had to be split for various Southern destinations, including 150 via Basingstoke and 200 each to the former London, Brighton & South Coast via Redhill and the former South Eastern & Chatham Railway via Redhill and Tonbridge. Punctual working would have been required to handle the extra traffic over this undulating route via Guildford, Dorking and Redhill, with possibly night opening of the line and new siding accommodation on the Redhill reversing spur.

In the end events caught up with this late manifestation of Outer Circle proposals; cross-London traffic fell and the block train for coal delivery and general traffic increased with the inauguration of coal concentration depots, Freightliners and specialised high capacity wagons for such trades as steel, motor cars and aggregates. So not all the proposed works were found necessary and traffic over such lines as the North & South Western Junction Railway and the West London and West London Extension Railways handles all the needful wagon transfers from the regions north of the Thames to Western and Southern Region depots.

Mention has been made of Freightliner container-carrying services and it seems rather tragic that all the depots for these are on the north-west, north and north-east sides of London. Planning permission was refused for adaptation of the Feltham marshalling yard site as a Freightliner depot. On the other hand, from the south and south-east there is not the mileage in Britain that would make an economic length of haul for containers on the railway.

All this makes gloomy reading compared with the enormous activity of the early years of this century, before the competition of the lorry had begun to bite. The number of freight cross-flows between the individual railway companies before grouping and still more before the rationalisation made possible by nationalisation, was such that a complete list would make as dull reading as a working timetable. It was exaggerated by the number of off-system depots maintained by the companies principally concerned in fostering the domestic coal trade with South London depots. These apart, the string of depots along the London & Blackwall line just outside Fenchurch Street–Haydon Square (LNWR), Royal Mint Street (two depots, Midland and Great Northern), Goodmans Yard (Great Eastern), East Smithfield or London Dock (Great Eastern), Commercial Road (London, Tilbury & Southend and thus later Midland) – or the thick cluster along the Metropolitan between King's Cross and Moorgate – Ray Street (Metropolitan), Farringdon Street (Great Northern), Smithfield (Great Western) and Whitecross Street (Midland) – were probably quite remarkable for any city in the world.

At my first school I had a friend who lived in a house backing on to the curve climbing at 1 in 99 from the North London to Gas Factory Junction on the London & Blackwall Extension. On Saturday afternoons between 1910 and 1913 we sometimes needed no other entertainment than to watch the succession of freight trains in both directions on this line. Great Northern 0–6–0 saddle tanks and massive 0–6–2 tanks headed many of them, with the scurling of the driving wheel flanges on the check-railed sections of the sharper curves; the North London was inclined to provide its 4–4–0 passenger tanks as often as its 0–6–0 T goods engines came on the freight turns on their way to Haydon Square. We knew some of the crews from seeing them at church on Sundays. I remember speculation as to whether one unusual engine (probably a London & North Western 0–6–2 coal tank) was LNWR or not; the North London usually horsed LNW freights, but there may have been a shortage of motive power occasionally at Devons Road depot, despite the NLR stock of 112 engines for such a short railway. The LNWR may even have exercised seignorial rights over its small subsidiary, especially after the consolidation of 1908.

Also from this wonderful vantage point, one could see Great Eastern goods trains *en route* over the London & Blackwall Extension Railway's viaduct through Bow Road towards the depots near Fenchurch Street or via the Salmon's Lane curve to the West India Dock area. Midland freight trains were on their way over this line to similar destinations. Looking in the same direction one would see the colourful electric trains with a chance jumble of cars in District scarlet and LTS green livery emerging up the 1 in 45 ramp from the tunnel under Bow Road, running past the substation and roaring over the succession of girder bridges across the North London branch, Campbell Road and the North London Poplar line towards what is now Bromley-by-Bow station. Behind us was the London, Tilbury & Southend route with 0–6–2 tanks on its freight occasions and its various 4–4–2 tanks with an occasional rarity resplendent in French grey (lavender) instead of the more usual green, which gradually after the autumn of 1912 gave place to the Midland red with huge gold numerals on the side tanks. Rationalisation of freight handling made havoc among the depots around Fenchurch Street between 1951, when Goodmans Yard and Royal Mint Street shut simultaneously, and the closing of Commercial Road (especially built for traffic from Tilbury Docks) on 3 July 1967. Soon after Haydon Square closed the site was a wilderness of railway equipment due for scrap, it having been rather hastily adapted as a place of security for lorries to park under load overnight.

The Metropolitan began its decline as a freight distributor rather earlier. The Metropolitan's own goods depot in the purlieus of Farringdon Street, proclaimed as the only depot in the country worked entirely by electric locomotives, was closed by the London Passenger Transport Board on 1 July 1936. Ray Street had, in fact, added only a very few wagons to the total of London freight accommodation. The Midland depot at Whitecross Street closed in the previous March; it was a small establishment with a short shunting neck on the level of the Widened Lines, with wagon placing conducted by capstan. The site was lost under the weight of the German fire raid on the north of the City in 1940. The Great Northern depot at Farringdon also on the Widened Lines, was the scene in 1932 of a big demonstration by the LNER of the work of the Mechanical Horse tractor and trailer in serving confined spaces. The depot had a spiral approach with several hairpin bends and narrow roadways between the rail tracks. The building sustained war damage but service did not cease until 1956. Last steam freight services to depots on the Widened Lines took place on 30 July 1962 with the cessation of Great Western operation at Smithfield, used just after the Second World War by that company to demonstrate its 'zoning' of provincial cartage operations. I remember examining the loading of vans at Smithfield for South Wales and following up on the following morning with a visual demonstration of the motorised cartage facilities in distribution from Cardiff to Caerphilly.

London has lost most of the goods and coal depots on its railways without the corresponding attainment of Gattie's ideal of a single central railway depot. The balance of advantage to the environment if that had been accomplished will now never be known, since we live in a short-sighted age in which any large capital expenditure is abhorrent while we are content to spend in total much more in capital and running costs so long as it is in sufficiently small dribbles, as with buying a multiplicity of motor vehicles, despite the ultimate costs of traffic congestion and pollution. We then justify it by the obvious platitude that 'the traffic had to end its journey on the road anyway'.

eight

THE JUDGMENT OF PARIS

With the persistence of Outer Circle railway promoters before one, it becomes relevant to ask if the peripheral attracts planners in other cities as a supplement to the radial railways. That some exist must be admitted; in Hamburg a circular service is operated, although with the radial projections from the circle the entire pattern resembles a catherine wheel. Moscow adopted a circular route which makes a centrepiece for that city's underground system. It may be noted that this was against the advice of the British expert whose services were lent to the Moscow authorities in the planning stages. This was Evan Evans of the London Underground group's staff (he was operating manager, LPTB railways, 1938–46) whose view was that circle services were full of problems, from timetabling to staff relief. At that time London Transport proposed to make the Inner Circle service discontinuous by a means which would avoid conflict with its statutory obligations.

Several cities in Europe have been building underground railways as relief to surface traffic by making public transport more reliable and free from the rigours of traffic congestion, and radial rather than peripheral routes have been chosen. Perhaps Paris forms the most striking example because nineteenth-century French thought was directed towards circular routes around the capital. The French main-line railways were constructed for the most part under a co-ordinated plan; the sectors radiating from Paris were divided between operating companies and on approved routes vital to the country, or 'of public utility', the State provided the way and works, leaving the operator to supply equipment and rolling stock. The sectors were for the most part so directional that several companies whose lines radiated from the capital eventually amalgamated smaller concerns and took up titles from the points of the compass – Est, Nord and Ouest; to the south-east the Paris–Lyon, which later became the Paris, Lyon & Méditerranée; to south-west the Paris–Orléans, which became the PO–Midi and the original Etat to fill up an area which did not appeal to the financial

[106]

backers of the other regional railway companies. Even with this ordered carving-up of the country some lines overlapping into the territories of others were built or acquired and had to be sorted out later. One penetrating line lasted until the 1930s.

Another defect in the system was discovered, and this was the same as among the unplanned railways of London; there were too few links between them. In the Paris area this was remedied by the Ceinture, which *Bradshaw's Railway Manual* prosaically described as the Paris Circular Railway and is now known as the Petite Ceinture. This was actually built by the Administration of Ponts et Chaussées, much of the cost being met by the State and the rest by five of the companies with termini in Paris. The Department of Highways and Bridges built viaducts for the Ceinture across the Canal de l'Ourcq and over the Seine by the Pont Napoléon, designed for road traffic also. There were also extensive tunnels needed on the east side of the city. But although 11 miles were completed by 1854 at a cost of over £500,000, similar difficulties were experienced in completing the circuit to those of London's Inner Circle.

Eventually the line on the Left Bank of the Seine was 'conceded to' (or forced upon) the Ouest Railway for completion. The entire line provided a route round the inside of the fortifications of Paris. Although it carried large numbers of people in the nineteenth century it seems never to have been operated as a circuit; the Ouest Railway always operated the service between St Lazare (and later Pont Cardinet) and Auteuil-Boulogne because this section was built by the Ouest before 1860 when Auteuil was counted as a town in the Paris suburbs and not as a part of the City of Paris. So when the Petite Ceinture was operated for passengers those making the round trip were compelled to change at Auteuil-Boulogne and again at Péreire-Levallois.

The introduction of the Métropolitain after 1900 made the Petite Ceinture less useful and the electric service from Pont Cardinal to Auteuil is all that remains of local traffic; on that section the business had declined from 33 million passengers in 1902 to fewer than 10 million twenty years later. The eastern section of the Petite Ceinture is used for certain through passenger movements from the Nord to the Paris, Lyon & Méditerranée and an important part of the action in Agatha Christie's *Murder on the Blue Train* takes place on the Ceinture, although despite the Calais–Menton coaches stopping in the Gare du Nord to reverse, that celebrated authoress made her villain board the train while it was going round the Ceinture! It may have stopped, of course; frequent delays plagued the passage of through main-line vehicles between one region andanother and although the remains of this Parisian Inner Circle have certain uses for freight transfers it is not surprising to learn that the Société Nationale des Chemins de Fer Français proposes new routes from the Nord to the Paris, Lyon & Méditerranée with the co-operation of the Régie Autonome des Transports Parisiens (RATP).

The Grande Ceinture circles Paris much farther out and as compared with the 32 km (20 miles) of the Petite Ceinture, it is 121 km (75 miles) in circuit. Several portions were already in existence before it was thought desirable for a line as far out as Argenteuil, St Germain-en-Laye, Versailles, Massy-Palaiseau, Villeneuve St Georges, Sucy-Bonneuil, Noisy-le-Sec and Stains-Pierrefitte, and it was not completed until 1883. The Grande Ceinture was built by a syndicate which issued bonds guaranteed by the State and the Nord, Est, PLM and PO companies. Later a Syndicat des Deux Ceintures took responsibility for management and payments on the bonds and this included also the Ouest company. The five companies were to divide the operation surplus of the deficits and provided new capital from time to time, as when the Grande Ceinture was provided with a stud of 0-6-2-2-6-0 Mallet tank engines for working freight trains over its heavy ruling gradients of 1 in 95. Subsequently 2–10–2 tank engines, built in 1925, were provided for Ceinture operations and then electric traction was introduced, first on 1·5 kV and then, for example over the 7 miles between Pierrefitte (Nord) and Noisy (Est), at 25 kV in 1959. With the development of large marshalling yards round Paris the usefulness of the Grande Ceinture for freight has risen. Of these yards Le Bourget (handling up to 2,500 wagons a day), Villeneuve St Georges (over 3,000 a day) and Achères (2,000 a day) are directly served by the Grande Ceinture and Vaires (over 3,000) and Trappes (between 1,500 and 2,000 wagons) are on the radial routes only a few miles from the belt railway, near Noisy-le-Sec and Versailles respectively. As a result freight on the Grande Ceinture that was just over 3 million tons in 1902 and rose to 10 million tons twenty years later, has gone on rising in the last few years, particularly since the rationalisation of railway routing in France since nationalisation in 1937.

Neither of these circular railways is greatly esteemed for through operation of passenger services. A scheme was considered for linking the Nord and PLM regions by a line across Paris making use of the bed of the Canal St Martin, built early in the nineteenth century and traversing the east side of the city from a basin at La Villette and then mainly by tunnel to the Seine above the Ile St Louis. It drops 90 ft at the north end, much of this by locks by Quai Jemmapes, but in the Temple tunnel on the east of the Place de la République it is straight and a level pound; it runs by an easy curve into the tunnel under the Boulevard Richard Lenoir. It has a width of 50 ft and the roof is 16 ft above water level. The canal is the end of a system still used for Paris water supply and another use is for building materials to reach the centre of the city by barge. This route was assigned by the Paris planning authorities for conversion to an urban motorway as long ago as 1966. Since then the SNCF has seriously considered the virtues of so much readymade construction (over 3 km out of 5) on the route of the link that is so much desired, between its Northern and South Eastern Regions, especially in view of the extra traffic anticipated across Paris by rail when the Channel Tunnel is completed.

Early in 1973, however, the SNCF gave up its ambitions for using the St Martin canal tunnel in favour of a link by means of the RER (Réseau Express Régionale) of the RATP. The co-operation between the Paris Transport Board and the SNCF is close and the RATP, armed with a greater independence from governmental authority since the end of 1972, is engaged in a heavy programme of extension, of course inside the framework of the national plan.

Of the projects in hand the RER is easily the most costly and is being constructed on a lavish scale. The line is designed to take full-size rolling stock (in contrast to the restricted loading gauge of the Métropolitain, designed originally as a metre-gauge system to ensure that the main lines would not be able to penetrate its tunnels) and stations are up to 125 ft below the surface, being equipped with numerous escalators and mechanical walkways (there are 73 escalators in Auber station), platforms up to 35 ft wide and shopping and restaurant areas; in some cases they are linked to underground car parks or new developments such as office block complexes. Stations are widely spaced – from Vincennes on the former SNCF lines from Bastille to Boissy St Léger there will only be stops at Gare de Lyon, Châtelet, Auber, Charles de Gaulle-Etoile, La Défense, to Nanterre on another former SNCF line on the other side of Paris – so that express operation is ensured.

The scheme has been a favourite project since at least 1930. As carried out it incorporates, on the west, a former SNCF third-rail electric line from St Germain-en-Laye to St Lazare as far towards the city as Nanterre and then runs underground through Défense to Auber. On the east it takes in a former SNCF steam suburban line from Boissy St Léger to Bastille, leaving it after Vincennes to pass underground to Nation. SNCF freight continues to operate to a depot off Avenue Daumesnil near the Mairie of Arrondissement 12. The RER is expected to be completed as a through east–west route in central Paris by the link from Nation via Gare de Lyon and Châtelet to Auber in 1977.

By that time a north–south RER line across central Paris will at least have been started; the Ligne de Sceaux, taken over from the PO–Midi company by the old Métropolitain in 1937, at present starts from Luxembourg and runs beyond Massy-Palaiseau (with a branch from Bourg-la-Reine to Sceaux and Robinson) to St Rémy-lès-Chevreuse. Similarly to the east–west line this is operated by full-size rolling stock, and after some vacillations on the part of the authorities it is to be extended, probably by 1978, by an underground link starting at the first station out from Luxembourg, Port-Royal, and avoiding the present outdated terminus to Châtelet, where an interchange station alongside the east–west line is planned on the site of Les Halles. These markets have now been removed to Rungis. The continuation north is proposed at least to reach Gare du Nord; to save the cost of making a new SNCF connection between the Nord and PLM regions, the north–south RER will be connected to the Nord main line; at Châtelet there will be three tracks for SNCF trains linking the north–south line of the RER to the east–west line; and at Gare de Lyon, where an underground suburban terminal is planned as well as an intermediate station on the RER, a physical connection would be made to enable SNCF trains to run on to the PLM region of the SNCF. Besides through services between the French regions of a main-line character the services through Châtelet will be 24 an hour on the RER east–west line, 6 an hour from PLM or Sud-Est Région to Défense and 15 an hour from the Sud-Est to the Nord, in addition to north–south traffic. A longer-term project, for which a joint RATP and SNCF undertaking has been formed with the object of financing it and carrying the work through, includes a northwards extension of the Sceaux line beyond Gare du Nord to give access at Aulnay-sous-Bois to a 13·7 km long branch from the SNCF to the airport Charles de Gaulle or Roissy-en-France. As the RER is equipped with 1·5 kV current supply (like the PLM), trains through to the Nord would have to be dual-fitted for 25 kV and 1·5 kV.

Each of the east–west sections of the RER are intended to throw off branches to the new towns that are planned for the Paris region and which are part of a French overall plan for that city to be a worthy capital of Europe and able to house a population perhaps as great as 20 million by the year 2000. In 1977 on the east of the RER it is hoped to bring the first part of the Marne Valley branch into operation as far as Noisy, leaving the line to Boissy St Léger in the neighbourhood of

Fontenay-sous-Bois. On the west a branch from around Nanterre on the St Germain-en-Laye section of the RER is proposed to serve Carrières-sur-Seine and Montesson. So, although there is seen to be some virtue in through routes across Paris, the idea of circular services seems in the 1970s to be a thing of the past as far as passengers are concerned, although the Réseau Routier of the RATP operates the PC bus service, on a route similar to the Petite Ceinture railway, aligned just inside the old fortifications. Parts of this service, especially in the southern arc, from Porte de Vincennes to Porte de St Cloud parallel a very old-established street tramway connection.

The former Métropolitain lines of the RATP, now the Réseau Urbain, were originally laid out on circular routes, but the circle formed by Ligne 2 between Charles de Gaulle-Etoile and National and Ligne 6 between Nation and Charles de Gaulle–Etoile has always been operated as separate lines and in fact Ligne 2 starts west of the Place Charles de Gaulle at the Porte Dauphine. Now the available money is being spent on improvements (the conversion of Ligne 6 to pneumatic-tyred trains was put in hand in 1972 to reduce the noise emission on the open-air sections) and on extensions of radial routes to serve newly developed suburban areas and even towns, sometimes so far from the centre that supplementary fares, above the standard universal fare on the Réseau Urbain, have to be charged. A typical radial route is Ligne 8 from Balard on the south-west via Concorde, Opéra and République, Bastille and Daumesnil on the south-east to Porte de Charenton, reached in 1931, and Charenton-Ecoles, achieved in 1942. At the end of the 1960s extension to the new town of Nouveau Créteil was begun and Maisons-Alfort Stade was reached in 1970, Maisons-Alfort les Juilliottes in 1972, Centre Hospitalier Universitaire de Créteil in 1973 and Nouveau Créteil in 1974. This extension involves a bridge over the Marne and a reversion to shallow underground construction through difficult geo-logical conditions at Carrefour de la Résistance and through a former quarry which had to be opened up and filled in to support the double-track tunnel. Although the loading gauge is standard with the rest of the shallow Métro lines, the stations on the new line beyond Charenton-Ecoles will take seven-car trains instead of five cars.

In 1971 Ligne 3 from Pont de Levallois-Becon to Porte des Lilas, which from 1905 until 1921 had operated only Gambetta, was diverted at Gambetta due east to Gallieni (Parc de Bagnollet), the section from the old terminal loop at Gambetta to Porte des Lilas being made a short shuttle. The Gallieni diversion was most interesting because the terminus there is in a building also used for a bus station (with space for

22 buses) and a 2,100-vehicle car park. It stands in a road junction complex that is the beginning of Autoroute 3, leading eastward from Paris and the planners are to be congratulated on this brilliant idea of making the underground system so accessible to motorists arriving by the motorway system, who would otherwise be forced to use a complex of narrow streets between Gallieni and Place Gambetta and to contend with the generally dense traffic of the French capital. As the A3 is extended to the east the value of this motorway-underground transfer will become more apparent. In any event the autoroute gives an opportunity for an express start to several bus services from Gallieni out to Gagny or Neuilly-Plaisance on the way to outer suburban districts. This underground–bus interchange under cover is an increasingly important feature of Paris and in fact the principal alteration to SNCF stations when taken over by the RATP for RER operations has been the provision of the elaborate rail–bus passenger transfer facilities.

Other radial extensions of the Réseau Urbain which are being examined are Lignes 5 and 7 to the north-east to Bobigny from Eglise de Pantin (5) and from Porte de la Villette to Aubervilliers and La Corneuve (7). On Ligne 5 there is a diversion proposed to the Gare de Lyon between Bastille and the Gare d'Orléans Austerlitz to improve the link-up with main-line termini on the radial routes. On this line great housing redevelopments in the 5th and 13th arrondissements (Panthéon and Gobelins) are proposed, with a possible extension south of Place d'Italie of Ligne 5 to serve the new construction between there and Porte d'Italie by a different route from Ligne 7, on its way to Mairie d'Ivry. Then Ligne 5 might go on to Orly Airport.

An extension of Ligne 14 at the south end is contemplated from Porte de Vanves to Vélizy-Villacoublay, over 5 miles beyond the old line of fortifications. By 1976, Ligne 14 will have reached Vanves. Ligne 14 runs into the city via Montparnasse to Invalides, a somewhat out-of-the-way in-town terminus for the underground where the Rive Gauche SNCF line from Versailles also terminates until such time as the SNCF has permission and funds to extend it to Quai d'Orsay. In the meantime part of this station has been used as a terminal for airport coaches. By 1976–7 the merging of Ligne 14 with Ligne 13 by Ligne 13 coming down to meet 14 from St Lazare should be effected. Already 13 has been extended to Miromesnil from St Lazare; it is scheduled to reach Champs Elysées-Clemenceau on Ligne 1 and from that new interchange to reach Invalides under the river is an easy stage. So a new north–south cross-route will have been completed on the west of the centre of the city. Ligne 13 is to be extended northward from Carrefour

Pleyel beyond St Ouen to reach at least St Gratien, so relieving SNCF suburban services from St Lazare and Gare du Nord.

Ligne 13 bis is also the subject of an extension project; this route leaves 13 at La Fourche and terminates at Porte de Clichy. From there across the Seine is Gennevilliers, with room for new housing estates. At the town end 13 bis might be separated from 13 by providing new tunnel from La Fourche to Place Clichy and thence into central Paris to Trinité (Ligne 12) and Chaussée d'Antin (interchange with Lignes 7 and 9); it would thus provide the stem of yet another cross-city route, but would effectively provide Gennevilliers with access to every part of Paris, even without the elaboration of a walkway under rue Halévy from Chaussée d'Antin to the Opéra-Auber complex of stations on routes 3, 7, 8 and the east–west RER. Other proposed radial extensions include projection of Ligne 10 from its loop at Auteuil westward to Pont de St Cloud across land cut off by the windings of the Seine but already to some degree built up.

So we are able to assume with some confidence that the close collaboration of the Société Nationale des Chemins de Fer Français and the Régie Autonome des Transports Parisiens is leading towards complete abandonment of the ancient equivalent of the Inner Circle in Paris, parts of which are a century and a quarter old, and to use of the Outer Circle solely for freight, while radial routes are developed and make to provide facilities for traffic exchange between SNCF regions as an incidental function.

nine

AS THINGS MIGHT BE

Plans for London railways are innumerable. Since the First World War major schemes have included the rather pallid recommendation of the Ministry of Transport investigations into London traffic, north, north-east, east and south-east, the 1935 plan of London Transport, the closely following, but non-published, plans evolved by the late J. P. Thomas after his retirement, the various post-Second World War plans of 1943, 1944, finally the working party of 1949, and then a series of London Transport projects as well as a multitude of private projects.

The Ministry public inquiries were held under the London Traffic Act 1924, the first, into travelling facilities to and from North and North-East London, under the chairmanship of Sir Henry Maybury, being held in October 1925. Three days were originally allocated for the sittings at the Middlesex Guildhall, Westminster, but public interest was such that it was spread from 19 October to 26 November. Now that the electrification of the Great Northern suburban lines of the Eastern Region is being carried out it is interesting to note a considerable reaction to the effect that electrification of the London & North Eastern Railway would not be sufficient and that a full measure of relief would not be provided unless it were allied to a scheme of physical junctions and through running with the Underground. Great Northern support of the Great Northern & City tube in 1892 did not materialise in such relief, and because the relations between the two companies deteriorated the original function of the G N & C as a City of London terminal for Great Northern suburban traffic is now only due to be achieved in 1976–7, a shuttle service only on the G N & C being anticipated by 1976.

At the time of the 1925 inquiry it was evident that the public disquiet centred round the change from tube to tram or bus at Finsbury Park. Although the LNER had plenty of plans for an electrification they had no money and an application for a loan under the Developments (Loans,

Grants and Guarantees) Act was characteristically made too late. The result of the inquiry was a recommendation to extend the Piccadilly tube to Manor House, where a tram station (also available for buses) should be built and for the London Electric Railway to explore the possibility of extending the Piccadilly Line to Wood Green or Southgate and the extension of the Highgate branch of the Hampstead tube to join the LNER at East Finchley. The first of the recommendations was carried out by extension of the Piccadilly Line to Manor House, where entrances were provided alongside the tram tracks, and Cockfosters; the new railway was opened in 1932 to Arnos Grove and on 31 July 1933 to Cockfosters, and this in itself eased the lot of residents in the Northern Heights to a great degree. The 1935 plan provided for other features although in the upshot some were never carried out.

The inquiry into East London traffic took place from 15 to 29 March 1926 and stressed the peak-hour overloading of the London & North Eastern routes to Chingford, Loughton and Ilford, especially the last-mentioned, where the situation was complicated by the London County Council housing estate at Becontree. Recommendations included electrification, especially of the Ilford line, projection of District Line trains to Upminster (it was noted that resignalling to increase capacity was already being carried out on the LMS-owned section used by District trains beyond Bow Road) and a revival of the idea of an additional railway to Waltham Holy Cross, partly underground and partly overground. At this time there was a very strong Ilford & District Railway Users' Association which made its views felt as a pressure group and produced detailed booklets outlining their proposals.

As a result the LNER was stimulated into producing at least four electrification schemes, the first in 1928–9. The first of these schemes did not provide for any additional tracks and only for limited resignalling. Sir Ralph Wedgwood, the LNER chief general manager, decided that not enough increase in carrying capacity was provided by these proposals so far as the Ilford lines were concerned. It was therefore decided to concentrate on Ilford and leave the Chingford and Enfield lines for later consideration. Three schemes were prepared on these lines in 1931.

These provided: (a) for electrification of the surface lines as far as Gidea Park, Ongar and branches (but not the Woolwich line) with a surface widening between Liverpool Street and Bow Junction; (b) for electrification as (a), with the addition of a tube for full-size rolling stock from Liverpool Street to just beyond Ilford; through tube services were proposed from Liverpool Street to Gidea Park and from Liverpool

Street to Fairlop and by a new junction north of Woodford to Lough-ton; and (c) for electrification of surface lines plus a standard tube ex-tension of the Central London line from Liverpool Street to Ilford.

The additional revenue to be earned from the tube schemes would not have been sufficient to remunerate the capital, but it was established beyond doubt that a tube railway to Ilford could be profitable *if con-structed by an outside undertaking*, although not profitable to the LNER because the traffic would be diverted from its own surface lines. For the same reason the surface widening scheme was not pursued with any relish by the LNER because it would have only provided a nominal return on the investment, although it would have been ample to carry the traffic. The LNER company never seems to have had confidence in its Essex countryside to justify it taking the view that clearing the clutter of suburban trains from the area out to Romford would have enabled attractive services to the Essex hinterland and developed it as a resi-dential area. The LNER board seems to have taken the view, having missed the boat after grouping, that there was room round London for only one Southern Railway in developing electric services far beyond the suburban steam radius, although to be fair the success of the Brighton, Eastbourne and Portsmouth electrifications was yet to be shown.

In view of the financial crisis of 1931 the LNER retained its attitude of masterly inactivity, but as the London Passenger Transport Board and traffic pooling came nearer, a 'window-dressing' scheme was evolved, with electrification out to Gidea Park, on the main line, Fen-church Street to Stratford, the Ongar branch and the Fairlop loop line (43½ route miles) with two new tracks from Liverpool Street to Bow Junction, a new single track thence to Stratford (for a Fenchurch Street–Stratford shuttle) and a second version of similar calibre but going on to Shenfield (totalling about 50 route miles). Widenings were expected to cost £3 million, plus £400,000 for colour-light signalling. The Gidea Park version would have needed 62 trains, including 10 spares. Of these 25 were to be new trains costing perhaps £650,000 and 37 were to be converted stock, costing roundly £1 million. The gross cost was put at about £7 million for the Shenfield scheme, and £200,000 was allowed for steam locomotives displaced.

The third of the Ministry of Transport inquiries under Sir Henry Maybury was held from 11 October to 9 November 1926 and dealt with the south-eastern suburbs. As with the two previous inquiries the time required was under-estimated, although in this case an interval was sought by the Southern Railway Company to consider evidence given on behalf of the local authorities in the area. The inquiry committee thanked E. C. Cox, chief operating superintendent of the Southern, for the very full and detailed information he gave and for the eminently fair way he presented his evidence. The Metropolitan Railway also came into the inquiry because of its interest as the operator of the passenger service on the East London line. It must be remembered that at the time of the inquiry the former South Eastern & Chatham lines had only so recently been turned over to electric traction that the evidence largely consisted of old resuscitated grievances without much regard to the current state of affairs. Electric traction between London Bridge and Croydon had to wait another couple of years from the publication of the report in 1927.

As a result the evidence was inclined to relate to the need for greater capacity of the Southern services and for provision of new tubes. A route from London Bridge via Bermondsey, Deptford, Greenwich, and Woolwich, returning via Lewisham, Camberwell and Southwark to the Elephant and Castle was mentioned, but admittedly there had been no consideration of it in depth. The London Underground group said the board had considered an extension of the Bakerloo Line from the Elephant to Camberwell under Walworth Road and thence via Dulwich and Crystal Palace to Penge and South Croydon; although the project, a pre-war one, had been reviewed since 1919, it had not been possible to give it serious consideration. In any event constructional difficulties were anticipated south of the Thames.

The recommendations regretted the closing and subsequent demolition of Old Kent Road station on the Southern, but because of the electrification of the Southern routes thought a Bakerloo extension beyond the Elephant and Castle the only tube railway project needing consideration. A link between the East London line and Southern suburban routes was considered desirable and an improved junction between the East London and the Metropolitan Railway between Whitechapel and Aldgate, to avoid interference of the East London service with provision of more trains to Barking. In all the reports provision of unified control of London railway and public road transport services was urged and this was eventually achieved under the London Passenger Transport Board in 1933.

The 1935 programme of new works, with Government assistance, followed on the formation of the LPTB and followed the lines suggested in these reports. The Central Line was to be extended from Liverpool Street to an interchange with the Great Eastern section of the LNER at Stratford and thence over the Ongar branch of the LNER from Leyton to Ongar, and the Fairlop loop from Woodford to Newbury Park was to be electrified on the London Transport third and fourth rail system. The two sections were to be connected by the new Eastern Avenue tube from Leytonstone to Newbury Park, serving Wanstead and the developing northern districts of Ilford. The LNER main line from Liverpool Street as far as Shenfield was to be electrified on the 1·5 kV dc system. A further section of the LNER, the Great Northern branches from Finsbury Park to High Barnet, Muswell Hill and Edgware was to be electrified for operation by Northern Line LPTB tube trains, with new connections from the Great Northern & City Line to Finsbury Park and from the Northern Line at Archway to Highgate, LNER. At the Edgware terminus the former GNR branch was to join the Northern Line and the long-planned extension from Edgware to Bushey Heath (dating from plans originally developed in the nineteenth century and allowed for in twentieth century road and power line planning) was to be built.

As the eastern end of the Central Line was to have a split service (to the Epping and Newbury Park directions) it was to be balanced by a split from the route to Ealing to run alongside the Great Western Birmingham line to Ruislip, later amended to Denham. Also in the 1935 plan was a new tube link, from Baker Street to Finchley Road, enabling a split in the Bakerloo service to Queen's Park and Watford by a connection with the Metropolitan Line from Baker Street, Bakerloo, to Finchley Road.

Owing to the Second World War these schemes were not executed in their entirety. The Central Line ran only to West Ruislip alongside the GWR Birmingham route when it was finished after the war, and the GNR suburban electrification was left at the stage reached early in the war period – High Barnet was added to the Northern Line and the Edgware branch was completed from Finchley to Mill Hill East. In 1950 it was decided that the planning restrictions of the Green Belt had robbed the partially constructed Bushey Heath extension from Edgware of its traffic potential. Had there been overall transport planning in Britain one might have seen it completed, with a car-parking area at the Bushey Heath terminal, as a means of diverting provincial car traffic from the M1 away from the Metropolis. Three years later it was decided that in the light of prevailing conditions there was no justification for the link to Highgate from Finsbury Park and the Muswell Hill branch of the GN suburban system, nor the connection for tube trains from the G N & C to the Great Northern station at Finsbury Park. The last passenger services between Finsbury Park and

Highgate ran on 5 July 1954. Freight services on all the LNER routes served under the 1935 plan were provided for by elaborate signalling safeguards and were abandoned in the 1950s and 1960s with the general closing on British Railways of wayside goods yards. For some time London Transport tube stock continued to be worked by battery locomotive from Wellington sidings, Highgate, to the isolated Northern City line, curtailed at Drayton Park after 4 October 1964 by the transfer of its Finsbury Park platform tunnels to the Victoria Line. After the 1935 plan J. P. Thomas, operating manager, railways, of the Underground, retired and spent some time at 55 Broadway on further new plans, some of which assumed concrete form during the war as deep-level shelters in tunnels suitable for a four-tracking of the Northern Line.

Post-war plans began to proliferate during the war. With very proper foresight architects and professional planners got together and in 1943 the London Regional Reconstruction Committee of the Royal Institute of British Architects issued an interim report outlining a grandiose plan for reduction of the main-line terminals to four – a Northern station to combine the functions of Euston, St Pancras and King's Cross, an Eastern station at Liverpool Street, a Western station at Paddington and a Southern station to replace all the Southern terminals. Each was to incorporate loops for reversal of suburban services and an underground circle was to follow roughly the route of the existing Inner Circle but with a diversion to the south side of the Thames to serve the Southern terminus. The Outer Circle was to be revived, mainly for freight, to link Kentish Town, Finsbury Park, Stratford, Bow, across the Thames to New Cross and Clapham Junction and then back over the West London route to Willesden. No estimate of cost or statement of the anticipated benefits accompanied the report.

It was soon overlaid by the railway recommendations of the *County of London Plan, 1943*, by J. H. Forshaw, architect, London County Council, and Professor (later Sir) Patrick Abercrombie, usually dubbed the Abercrombie Plan. Details of planning railways were to be referred to a special investigating committee. Elimination of steam traction was strongly advocated and the need was stressed for an organised freight circuit with properly planned freight terminals and receiving and distributing centres round the Metropolitan area. Radical alterations were proposed to the railway layout without much thought for the convenience of the commuter; while there is not much wrong with the idea of concentrating St Pancras traffic at Euston, the banishing of Liverpool Street to the site of Bishopsgate goods station and the conversion of Fenchurch into an underground loop terminal would have complicated the daily journeys of thousands. The conversion of Cannon Street, Blackfriars and Charing Cross to underground stations on a subterranean route from Deptford to Victoria and Clapham Junction, thus joining the former South Eastern and South Western sections of the Southern would also have effected a revolution in the habits of thousands, at vast cost. A tunnel from Snow Hill to Herne Hill was thought to be necessary to maintain the connection then given by the Widened Lines and the former L C & D cross-river link. No estimates of cost were given but it is typical of road-minded architectural thought that while railways were condemned as divisive of communities by their viaducts (the South London railway viaducts seem to have been under attack since the euphoria of the 878 arches of the London & Greenwich, as the greatest work since the pyramids, evaporated), viaduct roads were advocated to replace them. That Westway is more disruptive than the railway viaducts of the southern suburbs was only to be proved by experience over a quarter-century later.

Next came the plan of a London Railway Departmental Committee appointed in 1944 by the Ministry of Transport. The report, made under the chairmanship of Professor Sir Charles Inglis, was known as the Railway (London) Plan, and appeared in 1946. Although it was a high-level committee, with the general managers of the Southern Railway and the LPTB taking part in its deliberations, the desire to fulfil the planners' objectives of removing surface railways resulted in an impracticable proposal which involved nearly 50 miles of twin 17 ft diameter tunnels for full-size rolling stock; five deep-level routes came from a resited London Bridge station (on Tower Bridge Road) to various parts of London and were to be capable of handling 75,000 passengers an hour. Route 8 of the proposals was to link Streatham, Stockwell, Victoria, Hyde Park Corner, Euston, King's Cross and Finsbury Park to the Great Northern suburban routes of the LNER via Hatfield and Hertford to Hitchin – the germ of the Victoria Line concept. Route 9 in tunnel from Raynes Park via Clapham Junction, Charing Cross, and Liverpool Street to Clapton and the LNER Chingford line would also have incorporated some Victoria Line features. The viaduct from Loughborough Junction northwards would have been replaced by tunnel via Elephant and Waterloo to Ludgate Circus and King's Cross for passenger services and one for freight only from the SR yard at Hither Green to the Widened Lines. Abandonment of Charing Cross for a south-side station near Waterloo Junction would also have been included. Whether some of the intersections would have had convenient room in their subsoil for these proposals is a moot point that was not tested.

Before the Inglis Report was published the railways had been nationalised, and the British Transport Commission appointed a Committee, chaired by Sir Cyril (afterwards Lord) Hurcomb, its chairman, to review the findings of the Railway (London Plan) Committee in the light of economic and other developments. A Working Party was promptly appointed, with representatives of the Railway and London Transport Executives, under the chairmanship of V. M. (later Sir Michael) Barrington-Ward, to carry out this task. The Working Party paid much attention to the practicalities of railway operation and of the commuter's requirements. Purely architectural concepts such as removal of the Cannon Street, Blackfriars and Charing Cross railway bridges were therefore eliminated. It was the Working Party which recommended resumption of the 1935 New Works Programme, with electrification to Epping, Shenfield and Southend; quadrupling of the Metropolitan & GC Joint Line from Harrow to Rickmansworth, with electrification extension to Amersham and Chesham; electrification from Finsbury Park to Alexandra Palace, already referred to, and completion from Mill Hill East to Edgware and the new line to Bushey Heath. The 10-car train scheme was advocated for the South Eastern lines of the Southern.

What eventually became the Victoria Line was recommended as a deep-level tube from Edmonton via King's Cross, Euston, Oxford Circus, Victoria, Brixton and Streatham to East Croydon and a depot at South Croydon, with a possible branch to Walthamstow. This was listed as Route C and it was some years before David McKenna hit on the popular title of Victoria Line, in which he was ably seconded by Sir John Elliot, at that time chairman of London Transport. Route D was to be from Hackney Downs in deep tube to Liverpool Street, Bank, Ludgate Circus and Charing Cross to Victoria associated with suburban electrification.

Route F of the Working Party was from the Southern Dartford Loop and Sevenoaks lines in main-line size tunnels via Fenchurch Street, Fleet Street and Trafalgar Square to Marylebone and Neasden where the three $7\frac{1}{2}$-minute services proposed would split – one to each of the Great Central routes and one by a new connection at Kenton to the London & North Western suburban line for Watford and beyond, electrification of the latter being proposed between Watford and Berkhamsted. This time, supposing it was decided to abandon the railway bridge at Blackfriars, the viaduct would be replaced by twin 17 ft diameter tube tunnels between Loughborough and Holborn and via Euston to the Great Northern and Midland lines which would be electrified to Hitchin (by Hatfield and Hertford) and St Albans or Luton respectively. If there were an increase in north–south freight traffic potential, the freight tube from Hither Green under the Thames near Charlton to the neighbourhood of Canning Town would be justified.

While electrification to Southend (LTS) and by the Churchbury loop to Hertford and Bishop's Stortford was thought vital, with certain improvements on the Southern with electrification to Oxted, a low priority was suggested for extension of tube D from Victoria via the line of the Uxbridge Road to Yeading, doubling of the Northern Line between Kennington and South Wimbledon (with express service from Kennington to Tooting) and branches to Raynes Park and North Cheam; a westward link from Fenchurch Street to Bank, Waterloo and the LSWR suburban system in 17 ft diameter tunnels (route G), a projection from the G N & C terminus at Moorgate to Crystal Palace (Route J) or through New Cross to Woolwich (K) and extension of the Holborn–Aldwych branch to Waterloo (L)

Time alters the perspective in which new schemes appear. We have seen the Victoria Line materialise in the 1960s and London Transport has first given greater weight to the Holborn–Aldwych extension to Waterloo and then incorporated it, as we shall see, in the south-west-north-east scheme for a line across London. The Working Party plan for 17 ft tunnels for full-size stock, 26 ft diameter platform tunnels and 650 ft long platforms for 10-car trains, plus the 450 ft platforms on the 12 ft tunnel lines for 8-car trains was estimated to take 20 to 30 years and to cost £114 million at 1949 prices plus £100 million for improvements to surface lines, including the recommended electrifications. In fact in 1976 only the Midland line is a noticeable absentee from the proposed electrifications, and the Victoria Line, with a depot at Northumberland Park, joins Walthamstow Central to Brixton via Euston and Victoria by the quickest route across London. The first new part of the Fleet Line, from Baker Street to Charing Cross, via Bond Street and Green Park is well on the way to completion, but there is vacillation about the method of its extension, although to the writer the preferred arrangement would be to run via Fenchurch Street to New Cross and Lewisham, thus revivifying Lewisham and relieving a crowded section of the Southern Region.

Since February 1973, a committee chaired by Sir David Barran, appointed by the Minister for Transport Industries and the Greater London Council, has investigated London railway facilities yet again.

It reported at the end of November 1974, having carried out its work through a Steering Group and a Working Party.

There is in 1975 no lack of projects for making better use of some of the railways that have fallen into desuetude, even if some of them, such as the two branches from Nunhead (that is the Greenwich Park branch beyond St John's and the Crystal Palace High Level route) are irretrievably built over. The former London & South Western Railway line from Kensington to Richmond comes into this category between Olympia and Ravenscourt Park and in the same state are such spurs as the North London branch from Bow to Bromley-by-Bow, and that linking the London, Chatham & Dover at Snow Hill with the Metropolitan Widened Lines at Barbican, as well as the District Acton Town–South Acton spur.

At least two London Transport schemes are on alignments that could make better use of short sections of British Railways routes. Another type of London Transport scheme would enable a more intensive service to be given on existing branches of the London Transport railway network. Such a proposal is the Fleet Line, which by providing an alternative route to the point of bifurcation, Baker Street, of the Bakerloo Line, enables both the Bakerloo to Queen's Park and the former Bakerloo branch (now to become Fleet Line) to Stanmore to have shorter headways.

The first part of the Fleet Line from Baker Street was under construction in 1974, but the position of the rest was for the time being obscure. It should come into operation between Baker Street, Bond Street, Green Park and Charing Cross in 1977, giving valuable relief to the busiest portion of the Bakerloo Line by virtually doubling the service, but at the same time providing a new catchment area. At Bond Street it has enabled a much-needed rebuilding of cramped premises with a larger booking hall approached from both sides of Oxford Street and the installation of necessary additional escalator facilities. The increased importance of Oxford Street as a shopping precinct is thus recognised. The service to Green Park will provide a new facility in the rapidly growing business district of Mayfair. At Charing Cross the Fleet Line station will lie between the Trafalgar Square Bakerloo station and the Strand station on the Northern Line which will gain escalator facilities through the building of the new Fleet Line station. The whole complex will be renamed Charing Cross as both geographically more correct and to accord with the name of the British Railways terminus. Charing Cross on the District, Circle, Bakerloo and Northern Lines will be renamed Embankment eventually. The exciting name River

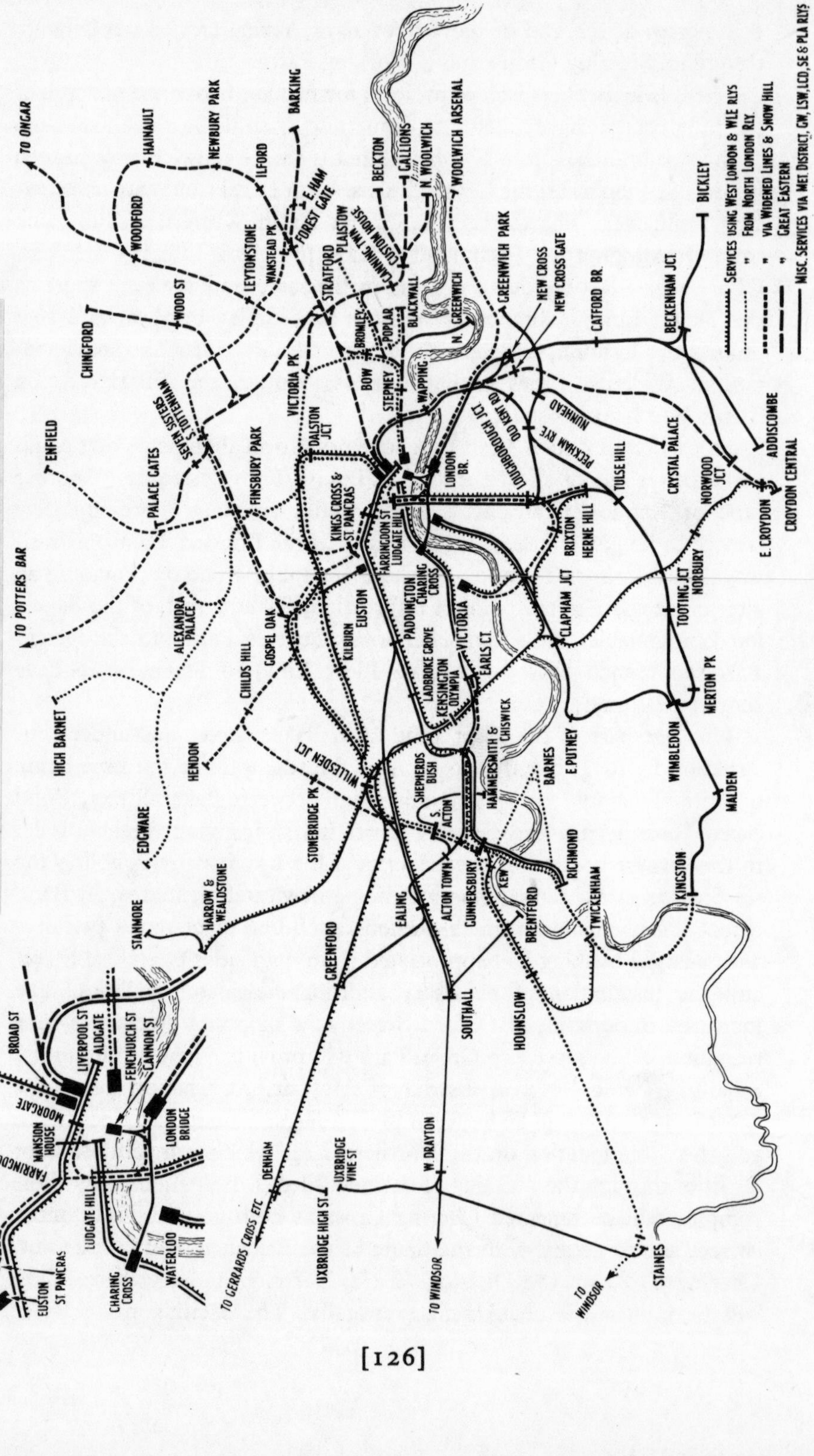

Map 2. London's lost railway services: Maps and services round London

Services using West London & WLE Rlys
" " From North London Rly.
" " via Widened Lines & Snow Hill
" " Great Eastern
Misc. services via Met District, GW, LSW, LCD, SE & PLA Rlys

TO ONGAR

HAINAULT
WOODFORD
NEWBURY PARK
ILFORD
BARKING
BECKTON
GALLIONS
N. WOOLWICH
WOOLWICH ARSENAL

WANSTEAD PK
E. HAM
CUSTOM HOUSE
SILVERTOWN

FOREST GATE
LEYTONSTONE
WOOD ST
CHINGFORD

PLAISTOW
STRATFORD
BROMLEY
POPLAR
BLACKWALL
N. GREENWICH
GREENWICH
GREENWICH PARK

ENFIELD
PALACE CATES
SEVEN SISTERS
S. TOTTENHAM
FINSBURY PARK

VICTORIA PK
DALSTON JCT
BOW
STEPNEY
WAPPING
NEW CROSS
NEW CROSS GATE
CATFORD BR.
BECKENHAM JCT
BICKLEY

TO POTTERS BAR

ALEXANDRA PALACE
KINGS CROSS & ST PANCRAS
FARRINGDON ST
LUDGATE HILL
LONDON BR.
LOUGHBOROUGH JCT
PECKHAM RYE
NUNHEAD
TULSE HILL
CRYSTAL PALACE
NORWOOD JCT
ADDISCOMBE

HIGH BARNET
CHILDS HILL
GOSPEL OAK
KILBURN
EUSTON
PADDINGTON
CHARING CROSS
BRIXTON
HERNE HILL
NORBURY
E. CROYDON
CROYDON CENTRAL

HENDON
LADBROKE GROVE
KENSINGTON
OLYMPIA
VICTORIA
EARLS CT
CLAPHAM JCT
TOOTING JCT
MERTON PK

STONEBRIDGE PK
WILLESDEN JCT
SHEPHERDS BUSH
HAMMERSMITH & CHISWICK
S. ACTON
BARNES
E. PUTNEY
WIMBLEDON

EDGWARE
STANMORE
HARROW & WEALDSTONE
CREENFORD
EALING
ACTON TOWN
GUNNERSBURY
RICHMOND
KEW
TWICKENHAM
KINGSTON
MALDEN

SOUTHALL
HOUNSLOW
BRENTFORD

BROAD ST
LIVERPOOL ST
ALDGATE
FENCHURCH ST
CANNON ST
MOORGATE
MANSION HOUSE
FARRINGDON ST
LONDON BRIDGE
KINGS CROSS
LUDGATE HILL
EUSTON
ST PANCRAS
CHARING CROSS
WATERLOO

TO GERRARDS CROSS ETC
DENHAM
UXBRIDGE VINE ST
UXBRIDGE HIGH ST.
W. DRAYTON
TO WINDSOR
TO WINDSOR
STAINES

Cross was, it is believed, tentatively considered.

From Charing Cross the Fleet Line is intended to follow the route suggested in the 1949 Working Party plan for a tube under Fleet Street, and should provide valuable connections with the south-west to north-east route at Aldwych, with the Southern Region Holborn Viaduct line at Ludgate Circus, with a complex of District and Northern Line stations by one between Cannon Street and Monument with escalator connection to Bank, thereby linking the Fleet Line with the Central Line and the Waterloo & City.

This stage of the Fleet Line would meet the crying need of a tube station to distribute passengers from the British Railways London, Tilbury & Southend electric service, by provision of a station at Fenchurch Street. Further extension is proposed south-eastward under the Thames to Surrey Docks, although the Greater London Council has put in a plea for an intermediate station at the St Katherine Dock site, now converted to housing, trade centre and hotel purposes. Surrey Docks on the East London Line could then become the terminus of that line's services from Shoreditch and Whitechapel and the branch terminal stubs of the East London to New Cross Gate and New Cross converted to be part of the Fleet Line. From the New Cross spur an extension would be made to Lewisham, where the London Transport station would provide for escalator connections to Lewisham Junction on the Southern Region and the Lewisham Borough Council shopping complex. This part of the Fleet Line would afford valuable relief to British Railways facilities from the south-eastern suburbs. A corollary to the setting up of the Fleet Line is the provision of a larger depot for Bakerloo trains at Stonebridge Park, the former London & North Western Railway suburban electric depot and powerhouse site.

A London Transport scheme for the 1980s is the south-west to north-east route first mooted in 1968. This would pick up the Wimbledon line of the District between Wimbledon and Fulham Broadway, presumably after segregation of British Railways Southern Region empty train movements to and from Wimbledon Park depot and provision of more adequate London Transport depot facilities than are available at the small and awkwardly laid out Parson's Green berthing sidings. The next section, no doubt designed for eight-car trains, would provide Chelsea with the King's Road tube long thought to be a major factor in the redevelopment of Chelsea, although if the precedent of the Victoria Line station spacing is followed there would be only one station in Chelsea, near the Town Hall. Another possibility would be to retain the District Edgware Road–Putney Bridge service and a service from the main stem of the District to Putney Bridge, giving possibly a more frequent service over the Earl's Court and Putney Bridge section and to take the new section of tube from Putney Bridge along the full length of King's Road with several stations, possibly one for interchange purposes at Chelsea station on the British Railways West London Line, but this would obviously be much more costly and over-supply the Parson's Green or Hurlingham area with rapid transit facilities.

The King's Road section would end with an interchange station with the District Line at Sloane Square and the new route would then parallel the District to Victoria, where there would be interchange with the District and Victoria Lines. The south-west–north-east route would strike off eastwards from Victoria roughly under the line of Horseferry Road to Lambeth Bridge where the development of the office complexes near Westminster Hospital would justify a station, with entrances about Marsham Street and on Millbank. The 'Millbank Line' might indeed be a name for this tube if it materialises; it is snappier and easier to convey than the Barran Report's 'Chelsea-Hackney' line.

On the Albert Embankment side of the Thames the new route could turn north to Waterloo, where there would be interchange with British Railways and the Northern and Bakerloo Lines of the London Transport system. An opportunity might be found in adding to the escalator provision of the Waterloo tube station to make a direct connection to the somewhat isolated South Eastern platforms (A, B, C, D) of the British Railways former Waterloo Junction station.

From Waterloo the next section of the south-west–north-east tube might be to Holborn, covering the long-advocated Holborn–Waterloo tube link and including the Holborn–Aldwych terminal stub left from the merging under Yerkes of the Great Northern & Strand (the original name of Aldwych) and Brompton & Piccadilly Circus projects. It will be recalled that a flying junction was apparently intended between the link from Piccadilly Circus and the line from Aldwych to Holborn, but whereas the completed Great Northern, Piccadilly & Brompton Railway had the northbound and southbound lines separated vertically, both Aldwych tracks approached Holborn on the same level; alas, the southbound Aldwych track is joined to the northbound Piccadilly Line track and the northbound Aldwych branch track is connected to a short terminal platform in the angle of the junction where the line from Piccadilly curves from under Great Queen Street to join the alignment of Kingsway.

Earlier thought about the Holborn–Waterloo link was that still in unmodified form the northbound platform from Aldwych could have been used by the shuttle connecting service from Waterloo and that the line might have been the place to try out driverless automatic trains where the queuing passengers would have been protected from entering trains except when gates on the platform edges permitted. As a part of a cross-London tube Holborn station would clearly need rethinking to enable cross-platform interchange to take place between the Piccadilly and south-west to north-east services. A new southbound platform tunnel would be a minimum requirement and although the differences in level could easily be overcome by the time Aldwych was reached, the length of the platform tunnels at Aldwych and Holborn would require modification if eight-car trains are to be provided. The depth of Aldwych station is apparently sufficient for the under-river passage to Waterloo and its position need not trouble us too much because by providing two sets of escalators passengers could be taken simultaneously to the north side of the Strand, an interchange with the Fleet Line and to an interchange with the District station at Temple.

A further complication in following too slavishly the existing layout of Holborn Station is that the Piccadilly Line platforms lie roughly on a north-south axis, whereas the next section of the south-west to north-east line requires a change of direction to the north-east, which cannot be made too abruptly if the standards of curvature adopted on the Victoria and Fleet Lines are persevered with. For the next station from Holborn seems to demand an interchange with the Metropolitan Line and this could be made either at Farringdon or to give a facility to the City Corporation's great living-in-the-City movement, Barbican. If attention is paid to the prospects of eventual south-of-the-Thames to north-of-the-Thames suburban facilities by British Railways, the connection would be made at Farringdon. This would have the additional advantage of needing less sharp curvature of the new line and more space before the next interchange, at Old Street. Important connection to be made here would be with the Eastern Region suburban services to the Great Northern suburban lines, using the former Great Northern & City 16 ft diameter tunnels for their function as intended seventy-five years ago; the Northern Line tube connection could also be useful for certain intra-London journeys.

From Old Street to the site of Shoreditch station on the North London line of British Railways is inside half a mile. This important road junction deserves a station on the new tube and no doubt the area could be a scene of Greater London Council redevelopment. The North London route station at Shoreditch was closed in 1940 and between there and Dalston Junction there was a station at Haggerston closed on

6 May 1940. Over this section, which falls from the viaduct across Old Street and Kingsland Road into cutting at Dalston, it is proposed that the tube trains should use two of the four tracks of the North London formation. The next part of the route of the south-west to north-east line would closely follow the North London Poplar branch through Hackney, and Homerton to Victoria Park, but the tracks are used for British Railways freight services to the extent that 25 kV electrification to link the London Midland Region at Willesden and Camden and the Eastern Region at Stratford and Temple Mills has been contemplated. It might therefore be desirable to descend into tube again to leave the surface tracks free for freight operation. It might even be an advantage to provide tube stations in the area without reference to the Old North London station sites. At Hackney there is little wrong with the position of the old North London station in relation to the shopping area. Further east the new alignment would give an opportunity for placing the stations and their entrances close to the gathering grounds of the customers.

In the present writer's opinion the operation of tube trains over some surface lines under the 1935 plan would have produced enhanced traffic if modifications of the station sites could have been made, especially at High Barnet where the old Great Northern branch terminus falls short both in height and distance of the shopping centre of the High Street of Chipping Barnet. Indeed, several other stations on the branch are cloistered in rural surroundings and such a traffic centre as Tally Ho! Corner is not on the tube. To have made a new line with stations on the Great North Road would have been tremendously costly, but it might have been more satisfactory traffic-wise.

From the Hackney–Homerton area the south-west to north-east line must burrow under Hackney Marshes towards Leyton and this gives an opportunity for a trajectory between the developing part of Homerton and the northern area of Leyton, away from the Central Line station and nearer the parts served by Leyton Midland Road on the Tottenham & Forest Gate Railway.

New construction would end at Leytonstone, where a rearrangement of the station would be made to provide four tracks and platform faces instead of three (with two in the converging direction from the Epping and Hainault via Newbury Park services), so that the new route could operate from the Hackney to Hainault direction without interference with the Central Line–Epping direction. This would enable Newbury Park and Hainault to have a close-headway service and provide for the Central Line to operate a full service in the Loughton and Epping direction. Physical connections would be necessary for service purposes, but the train services could be completely segregated and cross-platform interchange would be arranged for passengers who required the facilities of the other route and therefore needed to change trains. There is sufficient width of the ex-Great Eastern formation for the necessary tracks on the approach, but the northbound platform would require to be rebuilt for its new role, serving two routes in a station for the new line which would be a surface interlude in between tube tunnels. A new deep-level station for the new route would involve an escalator journey for passengers wishing to change trains, so that adaptation of the existing station would have the balance of advantage.

Headways on the south-west to north-east line, without branches similar to those used on the Central Line under the 1935 plan to reduce the frequency, could presumably be reduced at the thin ends by use of intermediate turnback points, such as Putney Bridge. Areas such as Roehampton and Putney Heath can probably be covered adequately by bus connections to Putney Bridge or such stations as Southfields. On the eastern end a demand has recently arisen for rapid transit service to the north of the borough of Havering at Collier Row and Noak Hill, but it is doubtful if these districts justify more than bus links either with the tube or with the British Railways suburban services, particularly if the open stock built for operation between Liverpool Street and Shenfield, with a mere 502 seats in a nine-car train, were phased out in favour of vehicles with more seats, which would reduce the exceptionally high proportion of standing passengers on the services between Liverpool Street and Gidea Park.

A more pressing need arising from the introduction of the south-west to north-west line is that of depot accommodation. The existing depot at Hainault could serve the south-west to north-east line on which it would be situated, but it might be desirable to provide new accommodation on the Epping arm of the Central Line for depot purposes, additional to the berthing sidings at Woodford and elsewhere. On the southern end of the south-west to north-east line the need for depot facilities might be a more substantial reason for making a short branch, although it is an area with much public common land which could hardly be diverted to such a purpose. The site vacated by the British Railways Wimbledon depot alterations might be adaptable although it is restricted in size.

Another London Transport line highly spoken of in Greater London Council circles is one to serve the possible housing areas made possible by the filling-in of inner London docks. Those scheduled are only

London Docks and the Surrey Commercial group, which to some degree may be served by the Fleet Line–East London Line developments. More distantly under investigation are parts of those in the Isle of Dogs, and the Royal group of docks. On an east–west alignment not far away from the axis of the Royal docks lies Thamesmead, the Greater London Council estate on the site of the Woolwich Arsenal artillery ranges which formerly existed on Plumstead Marshes. This axis might be followed from Aldgate on the north of the river, just east of the City, across the Thames near Woolwich, into Thamesmead. A more practical alignment for a useful tube (River Line North) would join the Bank, Liverpool Street terminus, Whitechapel on District and East London Lines, Stepney East (British Railways, LTS line), and then take up the alignment of the British Railways London & Blackwall railway between Stepney East, Limehouse, West India Docks, Millwall Junction and Poplar (the Blackwall end of this railway has been covered by a power station), traverse the area of Victoria Dock, Royal Albert Dock and King George V Dock by whatever way is dictated by the needs of the planned new estates, but probably by the Beckton branch alignment, pass under the river to the Woolwich side and serve Thamesmead as required. In the Barran Report the River Line South is favoured, as a more costly version which could combine some of the benefits of the Fleet Line to Lewisham and would run to and fro under the Thames from Fenchurch to Surrey Docks, Isle of Dogs, East Greenwich, Silvertown and North Woolwich and then back again to Woolwich and Thamesmead.

If this tube is to start at the Bank it might be coupled to the Waterloo & City Line of British Railways which could be transferred to London Transport management; there might be some difficulties of realignment at the Bank where it is close to the Central Line at about the same depth. By the link with Liverpool Street a valuable improvement in facilities from Waterloo would be gained. The Waterloo & City, second tube railway to be completed in the Metropolis, has 12 ft diameter running tunnels, a few inches larger than the 11 ft 8¼ in. diameter tunnels of the three London Electric Railway tubes, but the sharpness of curvature compels a limitation on the length of vehicles. It might be possible to remedy this if it was deemed vital to standardise rolling stock with other tube railways. At one time the interchange between the Waterloo & City and District Lines where their alignments intersect at Blackfriars was nearly made, but the proposal was never implemented – the Waterloo & City tunnels are on a 1 in 88 gradient; interchange does not seem so important today.

The River Line concept would enable transport facilities to serve these redevelopment areas ahead of the redevelopment works and is therefore of great importance. To the present writer the advantages of River Line North and entire separation from the Fleet Line seem to outweigh those of the more costly River Line South, which has not so much attraction traffic-wise. In either case an outlet westward of Fenchurch is needed and the Barran Report's linking of the River Line with the Fleet Line alignment is simply promoting the dichotomy experienced on the Bakerloo and Central Lines which the Fleet Line proposal and the SW–NE line is endeavouring to correct.

The extension of the Victoria Line from Brixton to Streatham is not included in the Barran Committee proposals, nor is the long-standing scheme for extension of the Bakerloo from Elephant and Castle to Camberwell Green and Peckham. Authorised in 1931, it was on the point of execution to Camberwell Green in 1949 but for high tender prices received. Of recent years it has again been a live subject for London Transport, in conjunction with a rolling stock depot beyond Peckham. In any event it would enable an improved service to be operated by providing an improvement over the two-track terminal at Elephant. It would also relieve some heavily trafficked bus routes – Walworth Road and Queen's Road Peckham directly, and other tributary thoroughfares.

For British Rail the Barran Report recommends seven electrification proposals:

1 Moorgate/St Pancras–Bedford
2 South Croydon–Uckfield/East Grinstead
3 Bishop's Stortford–Cambridge
4 Tonbridge–Hastings
5 Paddington–Oxford/Newbury
6 Marylebone–Aylesbury/High Wycombe
7 Basingstoke–Salisbury

They are listed in what is considered an order of priority for carrying out as existing equipment becomes life-expired.

The committee considers that the cost-intensive Ring Rail scheme, described in Chapter 6 (even though costs are probably under-estimated), does not show, on test, more than a moderate level of demand and thinks the stopping of main-line services at the interchanges would cause considerable time-loss to passengers, operating problems and loss of capacity. Instead it proposes a modest expenditure (£2 million) on making the North London more attractive to passengers and suggests non-radial services between Greenford and North Woolwich and from Clapham Junction to Barking. The first would run via Ealing, Acton, Willesden Junction (reviving a passenger link last used in 1912 for a steam railmotor service), the Hampstead Junction Railway, the North London line, Victoria Park, Stratford and the Great Eastern North Woolwich branch. The second would use the West London Extension and West London lines to Willesden, the Hampstead Junction to Gospel Oak and then the Tottenham & Hampstead and Tottenham & Forest Gate routes. A low-cost scheme would operate with diesel railcars at the end of their book life at 20-minute intervals; a more expensive version would give 10-minute electrified services and would provide a number of new stations, new interchanges at Willesden Junction, West Hampstead, Gospel Oak, South Tottenham, Walthamstow, Leytonstone, and Highbury. Electrification on the high-tension a.c. overhead system would require reconstruction of Hampstead tunnel. Other British Railway schemes considered are the linking of the ex-Midland and Southern lines via Farringdon; this is recommended as a priority of the second order. The diversion of Hayes and Addiscombe services from SR termini to the Fleet Line at Lewisham is proposed as Stage 4 of Fleet Line development.

Most exciting of the BR schemes considered for London is Crossrail. This would be a counterpart to the RER in Paris or schemes in German cities, with deep-level cross-London links joining Paddington and Liverpool Street on the north and emerging to the Eastern Region east of Bethnal Green; the southern tunnel would be mainly for Central Division services of the Southern Region and join the Victoria routes with the London Bridge route. There would be interchange between the two at Leicester Square. The northern tunnel would have intermediate stations at Paddington, Marble Arch, Oxford Street, Leicester Square, Ludgate Circus and Liverpool Street; the southern at Victoria, Piccadilly, Leicester Square, Blackfriars, Cannon Street and London Bridge. Such a scheme (with closer-spaced stations than the Paris RER) would reduce the demand on buses and the Underground and improve the terminal facilities for suburban trains by giving them a through run. It would be cheap at £300 million, but might be vital to public acceptance of the proposed high-cost daily licensing of private cars in London, along with other projects such as better interchange (Euston–Euston Square is cited) and covered bus stations at key points. Property development schemes, as at Hammersmith and Liverpool Street/Broad Street, might finance modernisation.